Soul Sister's Diary
Second Edition

© Copyright 2003, All rights reserved. Kathy L. Andrews, Cynthia D. Simmons and Crystal Johnson

---

No portion of this book may be reproduced without written permission of the authors and publisher.

ISBN 0-9710403-5-4

Printed and bound in the United States of America

For additional copies or information please contact:
JARR Simmons & Associates, LLC
P.O. Box 20659
Piedmont, CA 94620
510-872-8410
jarrsimmons@earthlink.net

Typesetting and cover design by
Per-Fect Words Publishing Company
www.perfectwords.net

Soul Sister's Diary
Second Edition

Cynthia D. Simmons
Crystal Johnson
Kathy L. Andrews

Any similarity between characters and
events in these stories and actual persons,
living or dead, or events is purely coincidental.
Some events may or may not be inspired
or resemble actual, real occurrences.

Soul Sister's Diary
Acknowledgements

We would like to show our appreciation to all the beautiful sisters who gave us their time and effort in helping to complete this project: Loren, Antonette, Caniece, Fern, Tonie, Katya, Dawn, Michelle, Nedra, Paula, and Jackie.

Here's to the wonderful people who gave us life, love and guidance. We would like to acknowledge our families and friends. They have all worked so well together to produce three talented sistas.

Thank you Alice Mae Simmons, Dianne Simmons, Regenia & Ned Taiste, and Abraham Simmons. Jannie Simmons, you are my heart. Thank you Martha & Earl Andrews, Kenny & Dee Dee Adeosun, and Monica Balogun. Shout out's to CJ Sr. and Big Dess - my foundation and light.

Sincerest thanks from Kathy (aka Nia Imani) to the International Black Summit body – you've helped me discover my vision & unleash my creativity.

Deepest appreciation to Cornell Jones from Cynthia - all those late night back rubs were not in vain.
Thank you for being there.

A very special thank you goes out to Laura Stephens and ReGina Bradford Tardy. Without their encouragement and support this book would still be a collection of notes on scrap pieces of paper.

Foreword

Under lock and key, our diaries from childhood shared tales of distant dreams, hidden ambitions, and fantasies of love's true requirements. As we grew into women the pages remained available for the sanctity of silent dialogue, healing and self discovery. With pen in hand, each blank page of a woman's diary begins to dance with a rhythm that is in-tune with her personal season. Her stories, and poems expose secrets, and exalt the depth of her hearts desires. Each jazzy, bold, sultry or quiet tempo reveals a sister's future accomplishments by looking through the window of her current struggles.

Women of color flow in melodic expression by the way we walk, talk, and view life's circumstances. In our core there is a precious tapestry of strength, courage and endurance loaned to us by sisters who have survived insurmountable odds. We have drawn strength from the archives of history, and intimate details of our personal experiences. For it is the power of unspoken dialogues that give the outside world a hint of our inner most desires.

May our diaries continue to serve as a springboard for self-discovery, boldness and tenacity. As each blank page discloses our purpose, dreams and goals the rite of passage will lead to a process of never ending freedom.

Table of Contents

Love & Relationships
- Perfect Ten 8
- Ghost Sister 10
- My Good Friend 12
- Girdles & Bras 14
- You Should Want Me 20
- Slammer 23
- The Beautiful Ones 26
- Ex 51
- Untitled 54

Societal Encounters
- Shopping While Black 57
- Diversity ? 59
- Stack the Deck 61
- Ghetto Booty 80
- Black 82

The Struggle
- Black Rage 84
- Chains 85
- Entitlement 87
- Respect to Black Thought 89
- Wannabes 92
- Voices 94
- Millennium Blues 96
- Public Safety 100

Spirituality & Healing
- The Third I 103
- Crucifixion 104
- The Lake 106
- In God's Hands 107

Soul Sister's Diary

Love and Relationships

Crystal Johnson, Cynthia D. Simmons, Kathy L. Andrews

"Perfect Ten"

Ever had a "Perfect Ten?"

Every time you think of him a huge smile comes over your face and your body comes alive from the thought of being near him. Tall, solid build, dark, lovely – just like you like him. Sassy, teasing, playful, pleasing – just like you like him.

"Perfect Ten" never has to say much. As soon as he comes near you feel rivers flowing, your mouth starts to water, and all you feel is passion.

"Perfect Ten" has you calling out his name on cold winter nights. The heat you generate thinking of him could melt icebergs.

"Perfect Ten" is like a panacea, solving the unsolved mystery, finding the missing link. Like heaven here on earth. He is always glad to see you and always ready to satisfy you. Smooth, from the tip of his head right down to his round soft rolls. His shadow leaves imprints on your body in places never touched by human hands before.

Once you find that "Perfect Ten" the addiction kicks in and you're falling like nobody's business. Complete euphoria, along with sleepless nights and losing weight. From the first time you taste him, you know no other will ever be right for you. Once you've been with a "Perfect Ten", it's hard to settle for less.

Soul Sister's Diary

It's not fair that he was only in your life for a short while. Why couldn't he be around whenever, wherever, and however you needed him? Lord knows you probably need him right now!

Ever had that "Perfect Ten?"

Well, nowadays my "Perfect Ten" comes complete with D batteries.

Soul Sister's Diary

Ghost Sister

It was my father's fault, spreading the seed without regard for consequences or feelings. It was my mother's fault, allowing him to abandon us for another lover, start a whole new family, a new life I was never going to be a part of. My sister's family, my sister's life.

My sister is out there somewhere. Without any intimate connection – we are both going through this life alone. It's hard, but not impossible, to try to build a relationship based on nothing more than sharing the same blood.

Our parents loved their addictions more than they loved us. My sister and I will have to learn to love ourselves more than we despise our parents.

How different would my life had been if I grew up with my sister? I may have had someone to share deep secrets with, someone to yell at for wearing my best outfit. We could have gone to all the movies, dances and concerts together. We could have shared stories of all the boys in our lives and shared the pain of all the heartaches they brought us. She'd be a constant companion for life.

It's so hard for me to accept that there is someone out there that looks like me. We share the same blood and yet barely know each other.

Ask me if I feel cheated. Yes. Absolutely. I feel cheated out of the precious memories I hear my friends talk about when they recall the days of sibling rivalry and camaraderie.

But it's my own fault for letting the past and someone else's mistakes imprison me. It's my sister's fault for not escaping that small town and the hypocritical folks there. It's our fault for not remembering the strength of our ancestors and allowing that strength to guide us into a healthier adulthood. It's our fault for allowing the lack of parental guidance to keep us from feeling good about ourselves.

My sister and I have tried to create a relationship. Distance, busy lives and lack of money make it difficult. Our personal demons make it near impossible. I understand what she is going through. I'm a few years older and I've been through the same tribulations. I've explained to her that there is no teacher like experience. I've tried to preach to her the importance of confidence and self-love, although I'm struggling daily to develop my own confidence and to love myself. I've tried to reassure her that I will be there for her and that we do, finally, have each other.

It's been months since our last chat. It's been years since our last hug.

Soul Sister's Diary

My Good Friend

"Hey Nicole, what's up for the weekend?" Karen asked.

"Well, I have a good friend that I'd like you to meet. His name is Lloyd. He is a sweetheart and a real positive Brotha'. You'd enjoy his company. He's very funny, smart, and has a caring personality. He is thirty-nine years old, sensitive, yet strong and determined. You know, part velvet, part steel, that perfect combination that every man should be."

"Sounds good but what's wrong with him," Nicole replied. "Go on tell me why he hasn't met anyone on his own?"

"Lloyd has definitely met up with some hoochie mamas. They seem to be drawn to his generous nature. One Sista' he went out with suggested he take her to Cheveche, a French restaurant in uptown Chicago. She ordered the most expensive entrée, a bottle of champagne, and had the nerve to inform him that she was saving room for dessert. After dinner, girl wanted and got a horse carriage ride through town and ended the night with drinks at the top of the Sears Tower. After Lloyd dropped $250 to please this girl, she informed him that she was still in love with her ex. She told Lloyd that after her ex gets out of jail, she is thinking of getting back with him. Some women are a mess! Oh yeah, Lloyd has had his share of negative experiences with relationships. He seems to always meet women that aren't good for him. I grew up with Lloyd. He moved to Chicago for his job for a few years but I think he is back in town for good. His family is from this area and he said he is looking to move back and settle down here. I think

you two would be perfect for each other. He is ready and mature enough to settle into a healthy relationship. He has nice phat savings account, he is looking to buy a house and loves taking long vacations."
Karen was giving Nicole the hard sell. She really cares for Lloyd like a brother and wants to see him happy.

"Alright girl, why me?" Nicole asked.

"You're his type! You are an educated, beautiful, black woman with a big heart. You are in your mid-thirties, positive and a real conscious sister. You have a great sense of humor. You're very nurturing and understanding. I'm not talking marriage, right away, but just a date this weekend. Come on, are you down or what?"

"Karen you know I hate blind dates."

"I know, I know, but you will like Lloyd. I would hate to see two great people not find each other. I love you both so much and I know this could be a good thing. Come on! Don't say no, think about it and I'll talk with you tomorrow. You and Lloyd are headed in the same direction and you should be heading there together."

"Karen, aren't you single?"

"Um, hum, I'm still single."

"Why aren't you dating him?"

"Well… he is not my type."

Soul Sister's Diary

Girdles and Bras

"Girlfriend, why are you trying to squeeze into that uncomfortable contraption?"

"Because I have a date tonight, can't lose ten pounds by 8pm, and I don't want William to see this stomach of mine. I'll save the horror show for our next date."

"Shit, you better show this William the real you and he'd better love it or leave it."

"Easy for you to say girl – you don't have an ounce of fat on your body. Brotha's today don't want healthy women anymore. That's why they are running to skinny white girls with no asses."

"Don't even try it! First of all, the weight thing is not why Brotha's are running to white women. I've seen plenty of those men with chubby ofays. So try another lame excuse on me."

"Chile, I got no time for your lectures. I've got to get myself together. I'll chat with you tomorrow."

"Okay girl, peace and have a wonderful time with William. Remember, always use a condom."

"Please, no sex on the first date. What kind of lady do you think I am? I have to do the bump and grind test first to see if it's even worth my time. Peace!"

Crystal Johnson, Cynthia D. Simmons, Kathy L. Andrews

Why did I tell Sandra that I was trying on my new girdle? Lord knows she can't begin to understand how this flabby stomach is standing between me and true happiness. Believe me, I couldn't fit into this Versace dress if my ass didn't have a girdle. Oh, and this miracle push up bra is the bomb! We flat chested Sista's finally have a chance at catching some play. Thank God, Tanika could touch up my braids last night. Pieces were falling out left and right. Nothing like braids and $65 to add a little length to what I already have. Shoot!
I have to make a drug store run. I don't have enough eyeliner and blush to hook up this tired face. Damn, the years sneak up on you so does the wrinkles and the few strands of gray. It's a good thing black women age well or I'd really be looking through.

Yes! These sandals are slammin' and go so well with the dress I picked up yesterday. I'll be turning men's heads and making their women jealous tonight. We all know the game; nobody wants you until somebody wants you. William, honey, you are going to want me. Oh shit, not if he sees these crusty toes. I wonder if Tina Chow's nail salon is open? I can get a quick pedicure after the make-up run. Good thing these tips are still hanging on from last week. I can't afford a fill until my next paycheck. When I get back home, I'll take a nice hot bath and put a little of the good bath gel in the tub. Yeah, I think William might be worth the good stuff.

Wow! I actually have a date on a Saturday night. How many women can say that these days? VideoHaus has seen my butt one too many weekends. And how many new websites can you look at without getting bored? I love my girlfriends but talking about men with them just makes me hungry and depressed. I was really starting to feel unattractive, like chopped liver or something. It's been almost a year since I had a real date. You know, the kind where the man picks you up treats you to a nice dinner or show, great conversation and all he is looking for is a little kiss at the end of the night or the chance to see you again. William is definitely the nice date type. He's got a good job and manners - his mama taught him well.

"Hello Miss, I was just wondering if I could have a moment with you," he said. Boyfriend looked too good in that double-breasted suit, his shoes were polished and not from Payless.

"Well okay, I am just having a quick lunch – it's so beautiful outside I had to take advantage of it" I replied.

"Yes, we have been blessed today with sunny skies and warm temperatures. My name is William Turner." He gently stuck out his right hand and I responded in kind. As we shook hands he smiled and it was mesmerizing, I felt my heart drop and butterflies taking flight in my stomach.

"My name is Denise Fullerton. Nice to meet you. Do you work around here?"

"No, actually I'm here visiting a client of mine, I work in sales so I'm out of the office a lot."

"Good for you, I'm trapped behind a desk and computer most of the day."

"Sorry to hear that" he said flashing that beautiful smile again. "Denise, I have a meeting and I have to run. I would love to talk more and hopefully see you again real soon. Is it possible to give you a call this evening?"

"Sure, my number is…"

I know, I know. I broke the playas' first rule, <u>get their phone number</u>!

- If you get the home digits, he may be legit.
- If you get the work number, be careful! Homey maybe hiding something at home, like a girlfriend or a wife.
- If you get the pager number, the man is dealing in shady business. Beware!
- If you get the pager, home, and office number, the guy is desperate – play him, it could be worth a few dinners, some clothes and jewelry.

Old William came through and actually called that evening and we talked late into the night. He gave me his home phone number too! He called again the next night and the next night. With each phone call he sounded even more attractive than I remembered him. He was a good-hearted man, working hard to build his castle. All he needed was the queen and I could play that role with no problem.

It's 6:15pm I'd better stop daydreaming and get my butt in gear. It's a good thing Tina's wasn't crowded. I feel a lot better now that the toes look good. I've got to run my bath. By 7:00pm I'll start the dressing process. Even though everything is set out, I still need an hour to put it on. Why it takes so

Soul Sister's Diary

long, I don't know but I always feel right after an hour of primping. Yeah, this hot water feels good. A bath is the best way to relieve stress. I shouldn't be so stressed; I've dated before. But, I haven't had this tingly sensation about a man in a long time. Yeah – this is going to be a nice night.

Damn it! People always wait until I get in the tub to call. I bet it's that nosey ass Sandra calling to see if I'm wearing the girdle. I love Sista', but she can be such a pain in the butt. Or, it's probably one of those stupid phone companies wanting me to switch to their rip-off plan. I'll let the answering machine pick up, I need a chill moment.

Beep!
"Hello Denise, this is William, I'm sorry but I have to cancel tonight. I've run into a little problem and it has to be taken care of right away. I'll try calling you later tonight and maybe we can get together tomorrow. I'm sorry!"
Click!

Did I hear correctly? Did William just call to cancel the date after chatting it up all week? Did he say he had a little problem and would get back to me later? Maybe the steam is getting to my head? I'll check the message when I get out of the tub.

"Hello Sandra, what's up girl?"

"Hey Denise, I thought you'd be on that date by now. What's up?"

"Boyfriend cancelled on me at the last minute. He is really lucky I hadn't tried to get into that girdle yet. I would have to hurt him then. Do you feel like hangin' for a minute? I'm not trying to be around if he calls back tonight."

"Sure, that new movie with that fine chocolate honey in it is out. I can't remember the name of the show but I know where it is playing. I'll swoop you in about twenty minutes."

"Sounds like a date. Peace"

Soul Sister's Diary

You Should Want Me

Long walks on a short beach, that's how I spend most summer evenings. Tonight, I need to clear my head and find peace of mind in the distant waves. I'm trying to figure out what's going on in my life, why don't I have a man to love? Why am I alone?

Alone, but not for long, as most Sista's can relate. Our beautiful black bucks, as sweet and as assertive as they are, would never leave a woman alone for too long, without throwing her a line. "Hello Sis." I turned around to see a distinguished and charming face.

"Hello Brotha" I called out invitingly, knowing all the while he didn't seem like my type. Um, nice body! Damn, it's been a long time since I've touched a nice body! I figured he deserved at least one minute of my time. I flashed that smile, the universal signal to men that lets them think, maybe – just maybe, I'll get some tonight! Without hesitation he glided smoothly into my personal space. God, he was so close I could smell the combination of cheap cologne and breath mints.

"It's not safe for a woman to walk by herself this time of the evening".

"Well, it's not quite dark yet. I live fairly close and there are plenty of others walking, so I feel okay."

"Well, do you mind if I stroll with you for a bit?" He puts on this half smile like please don't say no – somebody may be watching. I nodded pleasantly and we started moving towards the East.

"Hi, my name is Calvin."

"Hello Calvin, my name is Tanya, it's nice to meet you."

A soft handshake followed and those were the last words I spoke along our walk. It's not that I'm shy or reserved. It's not that I was in a particularly solemn mood. Calvin took my "nice to meet you" as a segue to running down his personal bio and life story without taking a breath:

> He's 35 years old - a Virgo - 6 feet tall - never married - no children - has an undergraduate degree in engineering - an MBA from Harvard - he makes six figures - he owns a house in the hills – a new Mercedes - he likes to travel and see plays – he's an excellent dancer and lover - he gives great massages - he cooks and cleans - he can stand on his head for over 5 minutes without fainting - he rescues small animals from trees – he leaps tall buildings in a single bound, on and on and on and on…

Twenty boring minutes later I begin to search my mind for the best exit line to say. Don't get me wrong; on paper Calvin had it going on! What woman in her right mind would pass him up, right? Thank God for a bit of insanity because in the whole time he talked, Brotha' never once asked me any questions about me. Typical! This man thinks that he is such a rare find that it's okay to pat himself on the back. His attitude said it all – you should want me. Running down his stats like he's on an interview, laughing at his own corny jokes, bragging about his golf scores, occasionally taking a few seconds to peep at my legs and breasts made him about as attractive to me as a big hairy monster. I finally found a lull in his monologue and went in for the exit.

"Calvin, it was nice meeting you. I have to go home now and make dinner for my boyfriend."

"Oh, you got a man?" The windbag's air has been deflated a bit. "Hey, can I get your number? Ain't nothing wrong with being friends right?"

I didn't see that one coming, think fast!

"I'm sorry, I don't think my (imaginary) boyfriend would like that, take care!" I quickly turned West and headed home.

Too bad Calvin didn't understand. All he had to do to get the digits was to show a little interest in where I've been and where I'm headed. Or, at least realize that the expressions on my face could tell him so much more than my titties and thighs ever would.

Crystal Johnson, Cynthia D. Simmons, Kathy L. Andrews

Slammer

Hello Ladies! After two years of celibacy I "almost" had sex last weekend.

I invited this twenty-four year old I met last Friday night over to my place. Had the fireplace going, brought out my trademark fruit slices and chocolate dip, and even had on easy access clothing. I rented the movie "Slam"; he is a poet and hadn't seen it yet. That should have been red flag number one!

Boyfriend rolled up with 4 bottles of beer, I guess he figured two each was enough.
That was red flag number two!

Black love was burning in the incense holder. There is certainly something sexual about fruit and chocolate. No man has ever resisted being fed fresh strawberries dipped in warm chocolate. After about twenty minutes, he started gnawing and pawing. Okay, forgiven. He was excited. Not to be conceited or anything, but I did look especially sexy that evening. My clingy silk blouse hung on my breasts just right, accenting the fullness of them. The matching silk skirt caressed my shapely buttocks and thighs.

Another ten minutes and homey is sucking and licking - cool, cool, I can get with that! After five more minutes, he already had the condom on and doing what he thinks is having sex. Jackhammering, powerpumping, and missing the mark at every turn. I can see I'll have to draw a bull's eye for him.

Soul Sister's Diary
❧

After a few more minutes of hammertime, I had to tell him to please slow his roll. He stopped, smiled at me and two seconds later proceeded again with the insane humping.

I thought he just heard what I said. I wanted to be patient, God knows I really needed some, but after another three minutes of jackhammer agony, my low tolerance hit its peak and I told him he had to get off me.

He said that his condom was too tight anyway, and it was the only one he had with him. Youngster wanted to continue without it!

"Have you ever heard of AIDS?" I asked.

"I'm clean!" he replied.

Red flag number three!

Needless to say, one minute later we were fully dressed and back to watching "Slam". Was it him or are all the youngins' like that?

For the rest of the night, boyfriend kept mentioning what a great time he was having. Lord knows I couldn't wait for him to leave. I plan to be unavailable to him for a long while. I had to ask myself later that night why did I invite him over? I couldn't help but thinking is there a lesson in this.

Lesson Number One:
Though they are cute, young guys aren't necessarily better at

sex and may require some teaching. Always keep a box of condoms and a copy of the karma sutra around.

Lesson Number Two:
Maybe God was telling me to stay celibate a little longer.

Soul Sister's Diary

The Beautiful Ones

Oakland Hills, California, home to a beautiful young couple named Jamal and Charmaine Walker. Jamal is a very handsome, conservative man. His skin is the color of deep chocolate and his smile is perfect. He played football and ran track in college, maintaining a 3.4 GPA all fours years. Very conscience of staying in shape, Jamal ran Lake Merritt and worked out at the gym on a regular basis. Standing at 6 feet tall and weighing in at a mighty 200 pounds, Jamal is quite the specimen. Charmaine carries herself well too. She always seems to have on the right outfits accentuating her petite, sexy figure. All the Brotha's complimented her on her almond shaped eyes and smooth cocoa skin. She wears her hair in Senegal twists. It is her favorite hairstyle, it is her crown and she wears it like a true queen. They both have good education, good jobs and successful careers. He is a lawyer with San Francisco's biggest law firm, Feldstein and Royal. She is an E-Commerce consultant at L. Henderson Consulting and works on the company's top account. Even their love and partnership is the envy of all their friends and family. Their wedding was truly beautiful. Over eight months ago, they flew their closest friends and family to the Bahamas for the nuptials. Alongside a waterfall, they pledged their undying love for one another. Mr. and Mrs. Jamal Walker, until death do they part.

The beautiful ones found each other their senior year at Princeton, and didn't leave each other's side for the next seven years. They were best friends, and even got along with their in-laws! Sounds too perfect, right?

"What happened?" exclaimed Jamal; "You used to cook for me all the time before we got married. It's 9 o'clock and I'm starving. Where is my dinner?" Jamal's twisted eyebrows and harsh tone shocked his new wife.

"Well, that was before I started working again", Charmaine replied hanging her coat in the hall closet. "Now I work just as many hours as you do. I get home at 9 p.m. most nights, if you haven't noticed. Do you expect me to have the energy to cook after dealing with those fools all day?" She could hardly believe it, barely one foot in the door and the first words out of his mouth were "Where is my dinner." After a long day at the office she was expecting a peaceful night. Any other night she would have found the strength to pull together leftovers from the refrigerator, but she was not going for it tonight. Jamal didn't respect the fact that she had goals beyond taking care of him. Everything was cool until she brought home a Christmas bonus that was bigger than his.

Charmaine quickly moved past the foyer towards the dining room and put down her worn leather briefcase. Sorting through the mail left on the table, she tried her best to ignore him.

"You know that is one of the reasons why I found you so attractive. You said that you would always be there to take care of me," exclaimed Jamal.

Charmaine slowly turned her head towards him and in a controlled but angry tone she replied, "What?" Kicking off her heels to give her toes some relief. "Does that mean I have to be your cook for the rest of my life? I'm working now, honey. How much can you expect from me? Talk about used

Soul Sister's Diary

to, you used to always tell me how beautiful I was, bring me little gifts and take me out all the time – so proud that I was your woman. Now it's about you and your Porsche, you and the fellas, or you and the TV. Do you think this is what being married is all about?" The client presentation and the new heels kicked Charmaine's butt today. Turning 180 degrees she gingerly made her way upstairs to the bedroom. Charmaine wanted to slip into her after work clothes and comfy slippers before she fell out from exhaustion.

Following close behind her every step, Jamal stiffened his upper body and pointed furiously at his pumped out chest. "Are you trying to say that I've been neglectful? Shit, when was the last time you let me touch you? Can you even remember the last time we made love? You are the one being neglectful in this marriage."

Charmaine looked at him with hurt in her eyes. "You are sadly mistaken if you think marriage is all about sex." Making her way over to the dresser, she pulled out an old Princeton sweatshirt and laid it on the bed. "You agreed we were partners in every way – ump, I guess not when it comes to cooking." She went into the closet and pulled out stretch pants. "Would you prefer that I quit my job or tell my boss, sorry I can't work late on that account because my husband is expecting me to have dinner on the table by 6:30?" Quickly replacing her stockings and dress with comfortable clothes, Charmaine climbed onto her side of the bed.

"It would be nice if you ever made it home by 6:30" Jamal fired back without missing a beat. "You've been at L. Henderson for several months now. Haven't you overcome that learning curve yet? I understand that you are finally happy with your work, but what about a personal life?" He sat on the edge of the bed, staring at her with his arms crossed waiting for her response.

Charmaine, shaking her head with exasperation replied "Jamal, when you worked almost non-stop on the Manning case for two years, did I jump on you for not being around? I had to plan the wedding and find our house practically by myself. I guess the double standard is alive and well. It's okay for you to work hard to get ahead and not have a personal life when necessary but when I have to spend serious hours away from home, it's a major issue!"

"Baby," Jamal said with a crooked smile and a softer tone, "How can we start a family if you aren't around?" He paused to let this sink in; he knows Charmaine really wants children. "You said you wanted to have kids…the time is right…I don't want to be an old man with young kids."

"Jamal, we are twenty-nine years old and we have plenty of time for children." Charmaine thought he was trying to be cute by changing the subject, but she wasn't going to let it be that easy. "I want to have babies with you, but right now, I'm enjoying the work I do. We can bank serious dollars and our children will have everything they need when we're ready to have them."

"Well, if you don't learn to put home and family first, what kind of mother are you going to be?" Jamal said with hostility in his voice.

Soul Sister's Diary

"I can't believe you just said that!" Charmaine was furious. She stopped to take a deep breath. Although she was much too tired for this argument right now, she couldn't let that comment go by. "Your mother worked her ass off to put you and your sisters through college and you have the nerve to equate working mothers with bad mothers!"

"That was different – we lost dad when I was young and she had no choice. She had to work two jobs." A solemn and lost look came over Jamal's face. Jamal rarely mentioned his father. Recalling the pain of losing his dad, as a little boy was too much for him to bare. "Mom always made sure we had hot meals everyday."

"We are living in the year 2002 and you are acting as if it's the 1950s. Your mother was a superwoman, yes. I give her much respect, but things aren't the way they were then. Men can share in household chores these days. It's not fatal for you to cook on a regular basis. I should have never spoiled you! I never thought you would turn out to be so old fashioned."

"I'm not being old fashioned, I'm just keeping it real! If your cooking was a part of the game to catch me, it worked but now I'm on to your game. Funny, how you don't know someone until you live with them."

"Oh no you didn't just say that! We've lived together for the past two years. For most of that time I was out of work and had time to cook. Talk about playing games! Are you forgetting the tired lines you used and the games you played to get with me? You're talking out the side of your neck and you'd better watch yourself!"

"Oh, is that some kind of threat? If you walked out today, I would hardly notice. You haven't been around anyway."

"You are so sad Brotha'. I'm trying to figure out how I put up with your arrogant ass all these years. You're an egomaniac! Your funky attitude is played out and I'm not arguing with you anymore. You need to sleep in the guest room tonight!"

"What? Why should I have to leave my bed? You'd better find the guest room, I'm not leaving!"

Charmaine flashed a look that could turn living creatures to stone. She silently got off the bed, turned towards the dresser, pulled out the first pair of socks she could find and walked out the bedroom door, without looking back.

* * *

That's it! I'll be spending a few days with my girl. I'll come home during lunch tomorrow and pack my shit. I need a break from his funky ass!

* * *

I can't believe that girl is being so ridiculous. She thinks sleeping in the guestroom is going to hurt my feelings. This bed is just as cold when she is here. I should break out on her butt and let her be without me for a while. I got it going on and I don't need this headache. Marriage changes everything! Women start wearing curlers and sweat clothes to bed. They stop cooking, but find a way to gain weight. We used to have sex all the time. Now she gets migraine headaches or is too tired. Doesn't she know that a man has needs? She seemed to understand that eight months ago before she got that job. Fuck her! I don't care where she sleeps; I know I'm comfortable. Jamal turns on his favorite TV show, "Sports Center" and turn his thoughts away from Charmaine for the moment.

* * *

Yeah! I am going to go chill with Yvonne. Charmaine fluffed up the pillows on the guest bed. She picked up the book her friend Yvonne left the last time she had an argument with her boyfriend and spent the night at the Walkers. I can't take Jamal's selfishness anymore. He owes me a big apology and I won't accept anything less. I always let him get away with his stupid little comments, but I never thought he actually thought marriage was all about taking care of him. I didn't get my MBA to sit around and play housewife. He doesn't want me to work long hours, but he likes showing off that Porsche. His salary alone isn't going to take care of our car payments, bills, and the mortgage. He wasn't looking for a partner for life, that ass wanted his mother and a prostitute! Well, I can't be a superwoman and I'm not a whore just hanging around to get him off. Boyfriend can't even keep it going for longer than twenty minutes anyway. Half the time, he can't get it up without excessive coaching from me. Shit! Sex with him is a lot of work, but if I told him that, his fragile little ego would break into pieces. Charmaine was too tired to read. She placed the book back on the nightstand and snuggled into the comforter.

* * *

She just doesn't know. I have many women pushing up on this! I'm a damned good catch and I should let another sistah get a chance at happiness since Charmaine doesn't seem to appreciate what she has. That little hotty at the office has been flirting with me big time. Yeah, I've been a faithful man for seven years to a woman who doesn't even want me. She just doesn't know, a Brotha' could die if he doesn't get enough sex when he needs it. It's been over two weeks. How long can I hear, "I'm tired. I have a headache." Or, "I'll pencil you in next week." This isn't a joke! I'm going to have to really cuss her ass out tomorrow.

* * *

Damn! It's 12:00 a.m. and I'm still fuming over his stupidity. I can't afford not to be on my toes tomorrow. You know those white folks at work make you work three times as hard just to throw you a few crumbs. Brian and Ned are always trying to take credit for the enhancements that I make. I have to stick around after hours just to document everything and double-check my projects. They stress me out enough at work…

> "Charmaine, you've done an excellent job for us and we want you to know we appreciate your work. However, you've missed several deadlines on the Snowin account. Regardless of what the web developers say, you are

ultimately responsible for their inability to produce and to meet key milestones. Well, we are sorry but we must hand over the account to someone more capable of being a good manager."

"Someone more capable of being a good manager," Charmaine gritted her teeth as she reflected on that day, "Someone more capable of being a good manager." Those words ring through Charmaine's head every time she feels like her workload is out of control. Now she often finds herself staying late to review the work of the individuals on her development team. Double and triple checking the day's progress so she won't have to hear those words again.

I got caught out there at the last company. I'll be damned if they play me at L. Henderson. Not happening! Jamal can't understand that? He knows what I went through before. This is my career and reputation, not just something I'm doing until I'm ready to have children.

* * *

Women are trip, especially black women! Jamal thought to himself in the darkness of their bedroom. They think that it's okay to treat you like a dog and throw you a bone whenever they feel like it. Am I really asking for too much? A little cooking, why is that so hard? Fix the meals for the week. I can heat stuff up! A married man shouldn't have to run back to his mama's house to eat. Everybody is going to start talking, "Can't Charmaine take care of her husband? Why you running home every other day?" God, I've got to get some sleep, it's almost 1:00 a.m. It's going to be a really long day if I only get a few hours of rest tonight. Turning off the TV, Jamal tossed and turned a few times and finally settled into relaxing position. Within two minutes he was out like a light.

* * *

Can't believe I'm on this cheap mattress. Men are a trip these days, Charmaine thought to herself as she twisted her body and tried to relax. Don't they know they are supposed to sleep in the extra room or couch after an argument? That's just how selfish that bastard is. I wish it weren't so late I'd call Yvonne. She can relate. Her dumb boyfriend finally acted up enough for her to get rid of him. I love Jamal, but he is really getting on my nerves. It seems like we're always fighting. I think my Christmas bonus had a lot to do with his macho attitude lately. I'm so exhausted from working all those overtime hours. I haven't had time to stroke his ego by cooking and sexing him up every night like before. I guess that is a threat to his manhood. The only thing he can brag about these days is his car. Men! Why does it seem like the key to their happiness is through their stomachs and their dicks? I'll call Yvonne as soon as I get to the office and break early for lunch to come home and pack. It shouldn't take long to throw some things in a bag for a few days at Yvonne's. Charmaine curled into a fetal position and quietly cried herself to sleep.

BEEP! BEEP! BEEP! BEEP! BEEP! BEEP! BEEP! BEEP!

Soul Sister's Diary

Oh my God, I hate that alarm clock! Charmaine quickly reached out from under the warm down comforter to turn the alarm off. 6:30a.m, it feels like I had two hours of sleep. Get up girl, get up! Charmaine slowly stirred her body around enough to gain full consciousness.

After sitting up in bed, it took Charmaine a couple of minutes to realize that she was in the guestroom and to recall the fight she had with Jamal. Damn! I'll have to go into the master bedroom to get my clothes. Charmaine wobbled down the hallway, stopped at the guest bathroom to relieve her bladder. While washing her hands, she looked up into the brass mirror and smiled. Last year, she dragged Jamal to an antique auction where they picked it out together. "That Negro never wanted to do anything fun unless I initiated it", Charmaine said in a raspy morning voice. After drying her hands, she continued on her way to the master bedroom.

Charmaine always got up first on weekday mornings because her commute took a bit longer than Jamal's. On any other day, she would be quiet as a church mouse. Today, she wanted him to know she was up and still angry. Charmaine barged into the master bedroom, opening closet doors and bureau drawers then slamming them closed with all her might. The banging, knocking and stumping was enough to wake the dead but Jamal kept still. Although she did wake him, he didn't move an inch. He was determined to ride out the noise and not say a word. And so the banging went on a couple of more minutes. Charmaine gathered up the belongings she needed to get showered and dressed and slammed the bedroom door as loud as possible behind her.

I can't believe that woman! I don't need any of her mess this morning, Jamal thought. I'll go to the office a little late today; I need a couple of more hours of sleep. He turned over, snuggled under the covers and prayed she wouldn't come back to talk things out. He didn't want to hear it, at least not this morning.

"Hello, this is Yvonne Gates" – Yvonne answered the phone in her most professional sounding voice.

"Hello Yvonne, it's Charmaine" Charmaine responded with little enthusiasm.

"Hey girlfriend! How y'all doing this morning?" Now Yvonne's down home country accent was coming out. Yvonne had been a good friend to Charmaine from the minute they met. After moving to Oakland from New Jersey, Charmaine found it tough to make friends. California folks were very friendly compared to back east, but friendly in passing only. They smile when they see you, say hello and will chat you up in public but rarely invite you into their homes or their lives. Most invitations were to get together at public social events or restaurant dinner outings. Yvonne was different. They were automatic buddies after sharing decorating ideas, discussing where to find good shopping outlets or a good bottle of Merlot. They met during "Happy Hour" after work three years ago. Charmaine was so glad to have a friend of her own since moving to Jamal's hometown. Before Charmaine met Yvonne, she only knew his family and his friends. Yvonne was her friend, someone she knew she could confide in and trust.

"Hey girl! I'm doing good, but I'll need a place to stay for a day or two." Charmaine waited for the inevitable "What happened?"

"A place to stay? What happened?" Yvonne said with much concern.

"Well girl, Jamal and I got into a fight. I really need space and time to think about me"

"Charmaine, you know you are always welcome to stay with me but you also know that running is not the answer." Yvonne sighed, "You and Jamal been together too long to let a little argument run you from the house."

Charmaine understood what Yvonne was saying but she felt pretty serious about needing some space. "Yeah – I hears ya' but if I can at least come over after work for a little bit? I would feel better."

"Like I said, it's no problem even if you need to stay a few days. My place is your place. Tonight we can try a little of the Chardonnay I picked up in Sonoma a couple of weeks back".

"Cool! I'll swing by after work. Should I call first?"

"Nah gurl, come on by, I'm going straight home tonight."

"Okay, I have to get back to the pile of work on my desk. Talk to you later. Bye. Oh, and thanks Sis"

Crystal Johnson, Cynthia D. Simmons, Kathy L. Andrews

"No problem – bye girl."

* * *

"Hey buddy – whazzup?" Jamal tried to sound elated.

"Jamal? Jamal Walker? Damn man, where you been man? Been a long time since you called me", exclaimed Reggie. Reggie the Rocket was Jamal's old running buddy from his single and younger days. They called Reggie the "Rocket" because he would shoot straight to a fine woman so fast he'd leave a trail of fumes behind him. Brotha' Reggie was definitely smooth with the ladies and he was always up to no good.

"Yeah Brotha', just wanted to see how you were doing, maybe catch up over a beer tonight or something?" Jamal didn't give a damn about what was going on in Reggie's life. The last he heard, Reggie was still working at the Post Office, living with his mama and dodging child support payments for the three kids he had from three different women. All of Jamal's other homeboys were married, had families and probably couldn't hangout on a Tuesday night. Reggie was the only person he knew who had no problems hanging on a weeknight. Jamal just needed someone to go have a beer and talk shit with for a little while. He definitely did not want to go home too early. Jamal wanted to hang out just long enough to avoid a similar confrontation with Charmaine. He didn't want another night of arguing. The plan was to stay out long enough for her to be asleep when he got home.

Soul Sister's Diary

"Cool man – you want to meet at Kenny's Tavern? The Laker's game should be on and that place always has a few honeys strolling through." Reggie always knows where the women are.

"Yeah man, Kenny's is cool. We can get some of them slammin' wings too. Save me a seat, I should get there around 7:00 – Peace."

"Peace out."

* * *

"12:45". I'll leave now and traffic shouldn't be too bad, Charmaine thought to herself as she grabbed her purse. I'll have enough time to pack clothes for a few days. Charmaine pulled into their three-car garage and nearly hit Jamal's old football trophies. Quickly breezing through the house and up to her bedroom, she pulled out two pieces of luggage that she and Jamal got as a wedding gift. She didn't want to give the impression at work that anything was wrong at home. Charmaine had to continue looking her best. Carefully thinking through the next three days she began packing her work clothes first. Then toiletries, hair care products, then after work clothes, then "just in case" clothes, shoes and then her sleeping clothes. There, I think that's it for now. This should get me through the weekend. Without disturbing anything, she quietly walked out the back door into the garage, carefully placed the heavy suitcases in the trunk of her Lexus and took off. By 2:05pm, she was back at her desk and trying her best to keep her mind off Jamal.

* * *

7:00pm sharp. Jamal hit the door of Kenny's Tavern and immediately spotted Reggie, in some woman's face, smiling, stroking her hand and pulling her close to him. Not being one for wrecking a playa's game, Jamal took a seat close to the door and watched the "Reggie the Rocket Show", grinning the whole time. Reggie is a master actor. If that girl only knew what she was stepping into, Jamal thought to himself, she wouldn't give him the digits. After watching the little slip of paper pass from her hand to Reggie's hand Jamal thought it was okay to make his presence known.

"Hey brotha'man", Jamal exclaimed! Giving Reggie the soul Brotha' handshake and quick half hug. "Hello beautiful lady", Jamal smiled at the woman Reggie just scored on. "Hello", she replied to Jamal, turning back to The Rocket she whispered, "Call me Reggie" in his ear and walked out of the bar.

" Hey man, I see you haven't lost your touch. Still chasing every pretty sista' you see" Jamal said.

"Can't help myself man, the ladies love me. Why should I be selfish and deny them the pleasure of me?"
They both cracked up and slapped hands on that one.

"I miss those days, man." Jamal took a bar seat next to Reggie and noticed they had a perfect view of the TV. "A few years ago, all I had to worry about was having enough money for a movie and a box of condoms."

Soul Sister's Diary

"Shh-h-i-t, I'm still worrying about that," said Reggie. "Child support is a mutha'. Brotha' can't catch a break these days, babies mamas always calling, needing money. Damn! When is it going to be my turn?" Reggie looked disgusted and angry.

"I know Blood. Women are never satisfied. No matter how much you do for them, they will always find something to complain about."

"Hey Kenny!" Reggie bellowed, "Get my man a beer and I'll take a Cognac." Kenny looked at Reggie with raised eyebrows and said "Who gonna' to pay for it?"

Cognac, why the broke Negroes always order the top shelf stuff? Jamal questioned to himself. Jamal signaled to the bartender, "I got it man, no problem." Since it was a last minute emergency call, Jamal thought the least he could do was buy the man a drink. He was prepared to cover the tab anyway because Reggie was always broke.

* * *

7:00 sharp. Yvonne just finished cooking Charmaine's favorite salmon and rice dish. Yvonne could definitely cook her ass off and loved doing it. Charmaine pulled out the bottle of Chard from the refrigerator and the corkscrew from the silverware drawer. Yvonne was like a real flesh and blood sister to Charmaine and her place was Charmaine's second home. Pouring two full glasses of wine, Charmaine handed Yvonne a glass. Raising their glasses, "To sisterhood", Charmaine said.

"Yes, to sisterhood and to an occasional piece of D on the side", Yvonne added. They both cracked up on that one.

"True dat, true dat. If it wasn't for the D, men would be useless." Charmaine said shaking her head and raising her Amen hand high in the air.

"Sis, that's all they seem to be offering these days." Yvonne said while sitting down on the dining room chair in front of her plate of food. Yvonne looked disgusted and angry.

"I know! It appears that there are more frogs than Princes out there. No matter how much you do for them, they never appreciate it."

"G-u-r-l. You know we done spoil their tired butts. It's so hard to find a good man who likes to do for you." Yvonne replied. "Oh, I forgot to get you a fork from the drawer."

Charmaine promptly turned towards the silverware drawer again and pulled out a large kitchen knife. Half-smiling she said "I'd sure like to use this on my pain in the butt man, but I'm sure someone would miss him and call the police on me."

"Please, you sure wouldn't get any D up in the women's prison". Yvonne joked and they chuckled.

Charmaine grabbed a fork and sat opposite her friend. After the second glass of wine and the satisfying feeling of a great meal started kicking in; they retired to Yvonne's beautiful living room. Yvonne definitely had an eye for decorating and

Soul Sister's Diary

Charmaine's bargain hunting tips helped her to have a "Lifestyle's of the Rich and Famous" living room on a secretary's salary.

* * *

A plate of wings, three beers and one shot of whiskey later, Jamal was feeling quite nice. Reggie talked so much about himself and his latest female conquests that Jamal hardly had a minute to think about Charmaine. As a matter of fact, Charmaine was completely out of his mind and he felt at peace. The Lakers were leading by fifteen points and the Celtics didn't stand a chance. Shortly after the third quarter, two sexy women walked into the bar and approached Reggie. One of the women Reggie seemed to know intimately and the other was obviously her friend. Attractive sisters, Jamal thought, yes, very sexy. A smile came over his face as he turned his attention to the sidekick friend.

"Hello Beautiful! My name is Jamal."

"Hello Cutie Pie! My name is Shawnte."

"Hey Shawnte, would you like a seat?" Jamal moved off the barstool to allow Shawnte to sit at the bar.

"What a perfect gentlemen. I really appreciate you giving me your seat. What else you got for me?" She smiled, sweetly and seductively, leaving Jamal spellbound and speechless. Damn! It's been a long time since I flirted with another woman, Jamal thought to himself. All of a sudden it was getting warm in Kenny's Tavern. Damn! I don't even have good comeback for that line; I'm really losing it.

"Hey man, my ride is here so I'll check you later," Reggie said, breaking the spell Shawnte threw on Jamal.

"What?" Jamal looked a bit puzzled.

"Yeah man, what you think, I was going to hang out with you all night?" Reggie smiled. "Meet my girlfriend, Cheryl". Jamal looked surprised, especially since Reggie just spent the last two hours talking about all the women he's been with in the past year. He never mentioned a girlfriend.

" Okay." Jamal extended his hand and shook Cheryl's very gently. "Hi Cheryl, it's nice to meet you. Reggie told me how pretty and fine you were. He's been talking you up all night."

"Oh really?" Reggie's girlfriend gave Jamal a great big smile. "Well, it was nice meeting one of Reggie's friends. I hope to see you again sometime soon." She and Reggie walked out of Kenny's Tavern arm in arm. Jamal shook his head and thought to himself, some people never change.

"How long have you known Reggie?" Shawnte asked Jamal. Sitting on the stool next to her, he paused and said
"Known that Brotha since we were kids, about fifteen years."

"Long time. I just meet him through Cheryl. Seems like a playa to me but what do I know." Jamal cleared his throat and offered to buy Shawnte a drink and she quickly accepted. Conversation between the two was light and flirtatious. She

Soul Sister's Diary

laughed at all of Jamal's jokes, touched his arm occasionally and gave him her full attention the whole two hours they talked. Shawnte finished her second drink and suggested that they finish their conversation at her apartment. Jamal was getting horny from all the flirting and wild thoughts of him and Shawnte rolling around her apartment butt naked. It's been a long time since he had a wild night of passion with Charmaine and the idea of sex with this fine woman was so, so tempting.

* * *

After finishing off the bottle of wine Charmaine and Yvonne were feeling quite nice. "Charmaine – won't you go home to your man?' Yvonne asked in a low and serious tone.

"'Cause, I need to teach his ass a lesson. He can't keep coming off on that chauvinistic tip. I'm really tired of it!" Charmaine responded with agitation.

"Well girl, if you want to teach him a lesson you have to play the teacher. Kids don't learn with the teacher being absent from class. Speak his language, talk in "man-talk", anyway you have to convey to him your feelings, do it. Talk about the issue from your heart. Jamal is an intelligent man and he loves you, he will understand. Go home and work it out together. Being in bed with your man is better than being on my couch."

Slowly nodding her head, Charmaine knew she had to agree with all that Yvonne just said. Running away from the problem is never the answer. After a few more minutes of chatting, Charmaine got her bags and gave Yvonne a big hug and thanked for being a good friend. Looking at Yvonne's hall clock it read 11:00. Wow! The time has flown by. On the drive home all Charmaine could think about was what she could say to make Jamal understand how hurt she really feels.

She arrived home to find the house empty, no Jamal in sight. Well, I guess he had the same idea that I did. Um, it just dawned on her that he hadn't even called her cell phone to see where she was all this time. Okay, that's okay, she thought, I'll keep that one to myself. No more arguments, we need to make up. Charmaine brushed her teeth and got ready for bed. Just like the evening before she reached for her sweats from the drawer but stopped short of pulling out them out. Closing that drawer she went to her special lingerie drawer. Yeah, I haven't worn something sexy to bed in a long time. I need to put on that teddy I wore on my wedding night. That may help making up a little easier. I hope he shows up tonight. That would be messed up if he stayed his ass out all night.

* * *

Jamal checked the time and it was 11:58pm. Wow! It was the first time in hours he actually thought about Charmaine and the fact she hadn't called him on the cell to see where he was. Good thing and I hope she doesn't ask any questions because she would break his neck if she found out he was flirting all night with some woman in a bar. He politely declined the invitation to go back to Shawnte's place. He knew in his heart that would only led to trouble and he told her maybe another time. "Okay, I understand, I'm sure your wife is at home waiting for you", Shawnte said while tapping her ring finger. Jamal looked down at his band and looked back at Shawnte like a little boy who got caught with his hands in the cookie jar.

"Well, we had a fight and I'm not so sure she will be happy to see me tonight." Jamal said.

"Nah, a nice man like yourself. Trust me, she's calmed down by now and she will be happy to see you. My loss." Shawnte grabbed her coat and headed out of the bar. Jamal couldn't help but watch the fine brown frame sway through the door. Damn! It's a good thing I love my wife! Jamal turned his attention back to the TV screen to get the sports update. "What! How the hell did the Celtics beat the Lakers? he said out loud. Kenny the bartender looked at him and shrugged his shoulders, "I can't believe it my damn self". Jamal pulled sixty dollars out his wallet handed it to Kenny and told him to keep the change.

On the drive home Jamal recalled the promise he and Charmaine made to each other on their wedding night. They promised they wouldn't allow themselves to get so mad that they couldn't talk things out. Charmaine is right, he thought. She was working it alone for two years. The Manning case was kicking my ass and I didn't know which end was up. Girl was by my side, staying up late making coffee and massaging my back. Whenever I needed her, she was there. For two years she treated me like a king and never complained. I'm being stupid; Jamal nodded slightly. I know office politics can be a pain in the ass. I have a good woman and I need to support her. I know I can be a little spoiled and selfish at times. I'm really trying to work on that. Cooking is not appealing to me at all. I'm not very good at it but maybe I can have her show me how to make a few simple dishes.

It was 12:20am when he reached home. Jamal walked upstairs and down the hallway to the master bedroom. "Honey", Jamal headed steadily and softly towards the bed, sat down next to Charmaine's curled up body, and placed his strong hand on her shoulder.

"Yes?" Charmaine murmured softly, half asleep but with a slight twinge of anticipation.

"I'm sorry baby. We need to talk this out. We promised each other that we would never allow arguments to go on too long." Leaning forward, he kissed her on the cheek.

"You're right sweetness. There is no need to get this upset and caught up in an argument." Charmaine turned over and reached out to hug her first and only love. To his surprise, she had his favorite thong lingerie. Jamal smiled and hugged her back. The warmth of their bodies heated the room.

"Jamal, you know that there are deeper issues between us. Issues we can't ignore. We have to work on this marriage and treat it as a real partnership."

"I agree", Jamal said. He kissed her lips, a deep rich kiss that relaxed their bodies and created a yearning to be close again. "We should take a mental health day today", Jamal suggested. "We have some things to talk about."

"Yeah, the way they've been slaving me, I could use a day off. Ned and Brian can handle things without me today."

"Good" Jamal undressed completely and slid into the bed alongside his wife. Our beautiful couple whispers sweet words to one another and made love until the sun came up.

Jamal and Charmaine eventually grew to understand that they both had needs that were being neglected. This couple learned in eight short months of marriage what most couples may never know. Listen to your partner with an open mind and an open heart. In love, beauty never fades.

Crystal Johnson, Cynthia D. Simmons, Kathy L. Andrews

"Ex"

When I woke up this morning, I thought of you
Of all the times we shared
Of all the places we went
And when I realized it was over, I cried.

When I met you, you told me you'd never been in love
I knew then, we would be.

When we spoke of marriage you told me
"I don't plan on getting married until I'm 30"
I told you "I always thought I'd be married by the time I'm 30"
While I was 29 at the time, somehow I believed we'd split the difference.
But now, you're 27 and I'm 33 and we're not.

I remember all the good times we shared.
The cliff diving in Jamaica
Oh, but we were too chicken for that.
How you helped me climb Dunne's River Falls,
Without you, I might have fallen, and without you
I have never, and will never climb again.

In Mexico, first Cancun, then Puerto Vallarta-
We shared garlic shrimp and Mayan ruins and lots of tequila in Margaritas.
I tried to match you drink for drink
In Puerto Vallarta I did, though you deny it!
But I paid for it dearly!

Soul Sister's Diary

And oh, the wine,
First in Napa then Michigan and Sonoma and Washington
And San Luis Obispo and Santa Barbara
We loved the whites, and together we discovered the reds
And now, your palate is probably a bit more sophisticated than mine,
But I still can get better wine in California,
Than you ever will in Chicago!

You helped me to fall in love with Chicago
Together we discovered new restaurants
And enjoyed old standbys,
From Cafe Iberico, where we had our first date,
To Jane's where we ate in and took out,
To the homemade Margaritas I served you,
Did you ever learn my secret recipe?

To the Mexican place around the corner,
To take out at Pizza Capri,
To your Jambalaya, and my chicken pasta dish
We shared meals, good wine and good lovin'
on Cortland street.
Not to mention the shopping sprees!

In the Winter, you preferred to go out,
I was content with a Blockbuster night.
But you managed to get me out in the cold,
Donning my furs
Although you preferred I'd leave them at home.

I loved nothing more than to cuddle with you,

Crystal Johnson, Cynthia D. Simmons, Kathy L. Andrews

On my sofa bed, watching a movie, or a Bulls game,
Or a soap opera, or falling asleep, while you watched a video.

When you decided to go to Michigan,
I had to leave Chicago,
Without you, it would never be the same.

So here I am, in California
Without you
And I will never be the same.

Soul Sister's Diary

UNTITLED

lying under the stars
i hold your soul captive,
with my thoughts.
i picture your smile,

soaking in the coolness of the grass
against my skin,
a reminder of your eyes
caressing my spirit.

as you sleep next to me,
in nature's bed,
wrapped in the protection
of your strong arms,

dreaming dreams of life,
hazy skies, milky way visions
fill my mind.
amidst the city traffic

that sounds with the rhythm
of a thousand whispers
a cool summer breeze brushes my face
like the feel of your hand in mine.

memories of this sweet
summer night
will last a lifetime,
traveling through our thoughts like a comet,

Crystal Johnson, Cynthia D. Simmons, Kathy L. Andrews

for a fleeting second
in the millennium
when we were once
cosmic lovers.

Soul Sister's Diary

Societal Encounters

Crystal Johnson, Cynthia D. Simmons, Kathy L. Andrews

Shopping While Black

I swear I will never patronize that department store again. They completely ignored me for a half an hour. The store clerk appeared bothered when I asked to try on the suits I wanted. He counted my items three times. I was holding two suits and one blouse, but he had to make sure there wasn't an extra blouse or a pair of shoes hidden somewhere in the clothing. If it weren't illegal, I'm sure he would have patted me down too.

God, it doesn't matter what I wear, whom I'm with or the time of day. One of these two things always happens when I'm shopping; either I'm ignored or I'm watched! On this day, the security guard did the latter.

I chose to ignore the guard's gaze. The sad truth is I am so used to having the guards follow me while I'm shopping that it doesn't even faze me anymore. After ten minutes in a store, if I don't see a guard, I start to wonder where he is. I see another Sista' checking out the dress rack next to me. The guard probably assumes we are working together on some sort of "boost".

At the dressing room, Count Dracula hands me a plastic ring with the number five on it. The Count uses special black woman math - two suits count as four items? Is that how it goes? Would he count them that way if I were white?

After trying the suits on, I picked the one that accented my slim waist and de-emphasized my big thighs. The color looked fantastic against my rich, dark skin. And I didn't even have to have the jacket taken in to fit my size eight upper body or the hips let out to fit my size ten butt.

I handed my Platinum MasterCard to Count Dracula and he examined it like an auditor from the IRS. Would staring at the card enable him to see whether this $199 suit, plus tax, would put me near my maximum limit? I sent the last payment in on time to make this purchase stress free. Of course, he "needed' to see valid ID. After I give him my license, he marks something on the store's receipt. The count asked for my phone number. "Store policy," he says. I know better than that and told him I wasn't going to provide that information. Dracula just made a screw face and continued to process the transaction. There was no "thank you", no "come again", and no offer of discount coupons. He offered them to the white woman ahead of me in line. I swear I will never patronize this department store again.

My pride should have taken me out of that store when the clerk got funky the first time. I should have taken the time to report him to the manager. His lousy treatment should have been enough to turn me off from shopping at department stores for awhile. It was a beautiful suit rung up by an ignorant and ugly clerk. No suit is worth the experience of being degraded. I don't deserve to be treated like a second-class citizen or a criminal. No suit should cost you your self-respect. But where else can I find a beautiful suit like this for only $199?

Crystal Johnson, Cynthia D. Simmons, Kathy L. Andrews

Diversity?

Walking down the streets of major cities across the U.S., we see brown, white, yellow, red, and black bodies hustling to make a living, trying to pull that green. Green is the most important color of them all. If you have green, you are respected and revered in America. Unless you are black or brown and trying to catch a cab late at night or shopping in certain malls in certain towns, or driving an expensive car in expensive neighborhoods, you'll soon realize that not everyone thinks brown or black goes well with green.

Hustle! The hustle will pay off, they tell you. When you bust out the right grades to gain entrance into that red brick university, draped in green ivy, only to feel like you made the wrong choice. For all four years, they tell you that you only made it there because they had to change the pristine white institution into a white institution mixed with a little brown, a lot of yellow, some red, and a pinch of black.

Once you are on campus, there are no reflections of your heritage, traditions, or culture anywhere. The color of your skin isolates you from the mainstream.

Years later, you are armed with the off-white sheepskin paper that cost you $80,000 in loans, and reads: "Now, you have a brain, scarecrow. You can leave OZ and enter the real world, prepared!" Prepared to make tall green and hoping to suffer less blues then your parents did. But they didn't prepare you for the conspiracy, the red, white, and blue cover up, and the insecurities that plague corporate Americans. Those other folks who were there before you are waiting to be envious of

Soul Sister's Diary

your achievements, your knowledge and your attitude. Attitude, yeah that's her problem. She has an attitude problem; she is impossible to work with. Funny, the last person of color working in this office was fired for having attitude.

Diversity means there are a few browns, reds, yellows and blacks sprinkled carefully among a field of whites. Diversity means that minorities make up the majority of low paying jobs in most major companies. They say there is diversity in America. Then why are we still honoring the first Black, Latino, Asian, Native American this and that in highly visible social and political arenas?

Today, when you walk down the streets of every major city you can see fewer browns, yellows, reds, and blacks and more whites. Yeah, whites are moving in, moving back, and taking over the inner city. The neighborhoods are becoming cleaner, safer, and more expensive. It's a miracle! Browns, reds, yellows and blacks are finally getting those home loans, but only if their homes are outside the city.

When the economy is booming, there is green to be made. Green gets you where you want to be unless you are black or brown. Not everyone thinks black or brown could possibly go well with green.

Crystal Johnson, Cynthia D. Simmons, Kathy L. Andrews

Stack The Deck

Candace Williams was having a great day. She'd just wrapped up the Wilkes-Rogers audit in record time and her client and her Senior Manager were extremely pleased with her work. As a result she was a shoo in for her eagerly sought after promotion to audit Manager at Young & Towne. Candace was truly blessed. She was 5' 9", slender with smooth, caramel-colored skin and a radiant smile. She was often mistaken for a model. Candace had large, round light-brown eyes, and shoulder-length hair, which she usually wore pulled pack in a bun for work.

Young & Towne was a big five accounting firm with offices worldwide. With company headquarters in Chicago, Y&T was clearly the most prestigious firm in the windy city. At 25, Candace would be the youngest person ever to be promoted to Manager in the Chicago Office, perhaps in the entire firm. She would have the dual honor of being Y&T's first black female Manager. Y&T should have been ashamed to admit that in 2001, they would finally be promoting a black woman to this position. After all, Maurice Hill had broken the color barrier way back in 1975, but black women never seemed to be able to make it through the ranks. Of course, during the 1980s and 1990s when careers in public accounting lost their cache to investment banking and consulting professions, there were a lot less sisters pursuing these positions. When the go-go economy of the 1990s started slowing in the new millennium, there was renewed interest in a stable, even if a relatively boring profession, like accounting.

Soul Sister's Diary

While Candace was in her sophomore year working on her undergraduate business degree at Wharton, she had taken the advice of one the few black professors. "Get a good solid foundation in something like accounting," Professor Jackson had advised, "then you'll be set to pursue some of the more sexy, lucrative professions later, after graduate school. No matter what happens in business, the world will always need good accountants." In 2001, Candace watched with horror as many of her friends, who'd gone to work for dot.coms or big, prestigious consulting firms got laid off. She silently thanked the creator for putting Professor Jackson in her path. She also silently thanked the sisters who'd come before her paving her way.

Things hadn't always gone smoothly at Y&T. In fact, Candace couldn't remember a time in the last four years since she'd joined the firm when she had been this happy. Circumstances were still far from perfect, but after four years it looked like she'd finally overcome her rocky start. When Candace joined Y&T, she was shocked to find out that she was the only black female in the Chicago office's Audit department. During the interview process, she had met two other black women. Apparently, the summer before Candace started the other women had left, much to her dismay. When Candace asked around as to what had happened to them, no one was willing to talk about it. Unfortunately, Candace didn't have home phone numbers for either of the women, and the Human Resources department wouldn't give out the information. Eventually, Candace ran into one of them, Sandra Wright, at a National Association for Black Accountants (NABA) luncheon, and the two got a chance to talk.

Sandra warned Candace that Y&T was not an easy place for blacks to work, and that she and Bernice had left because they were passed over for promotion to Manager. Apparently, no black person since Maurice Hill had ever made it beyond senior, Candace's current position, in the Chicago office. Sandra and Bernice had both been doing quite well up until their last year. Then suddenly, they couldn't do anything right. Since the evaluation process was somewhat subjective at Young & Towne, it was difficult for them to prove that the firm's actions were racially motivated. Nonetheless, they had decided to jointly file a lawsuit. When their lawyers had contacted the Managers and Partners for whom they had worked, all of whom had given them good evaluations, every single one of them indicated that they would not support Sandra and Bernice in their lawsuit. They all claimed that each audit is different and thus, while Sandra and Bernice had performed adequately on their engagements, this did not demonstrate that they were qualified for promotion to Manager. Fortunately, both Sandra and Bernice had developed strong relationships with their clients and thus had some witnesses who were willing to go for bat for them. However, their attorney suggested that the evidence wasn't strong enough to support a discrimination claim, and advised them it wouldn't be worth it to go through with a long, expensive court battle without the support of their former Managers. Y&T was savvy enough to not want to risk the bad press, so they did offer monetary settlements. No amount of money they could pay Sandra and Bernice, however, could assuage the pain the two had suffered at the hands of Y&T. Candace felt truly sorry for what the sisters had suffered and vowed from that day on that she would not go out like that. Sandra and Bernice had bounced back nicely; both getting lucrative offers to join the accounting staffs of their former audit clients, so it ended well. Still, Y&T had some nerve playing games

Soul Sister's Diary

with the lives and careers of such talented sisters.

Forewarned meant forearmed, and sure enough Candace had run into racism at Young & Towne from the start. On her first audit engagement, Candace had been assigned to work with Andy, a fairly ordinary white guy who had recently moved to Chicago from South Carolina. Andy was a blonde haired, blue-eyed devil, with a strong southern drawl that irritated Candace more than fingernails scraping on a chalkboard. Perhaps because he had grown up in the south, he had developed an inbred loathing of black folks. Candace wasn't sure, but whatever the case, Andy did not like Candace. On their first day together he had the nerve to tell her that he knew the only reason she got the job was because of Affirmative Action. But Candace was no ordinary sister. To say she was an overachiever would be a vast understatement. When she pointed out to him that she'd graduated from Wharton, one of the top undergraduate business programs, while he had finished in the middle of his class at South Carolina State, he responded that she probably only got into Wharton because she was a minority. Candace conceded that while it was possible that Affirmative Action had contributed to her admission at Wharton, it did not account for her stellar performance there. She hated to toot her own horn, but found it necessary to inform him that she had finished in the top 5% of her class. While that shut him up, at least temporarily, it also set the tone for the entire audit. It seemed that throughout the audit, he constantly tried to trip her up. When she had a question, he'd say "you're so smart, figure it out." When he reviewed her work, he'd give her vague and unhelpful feedback. His whole attitude toward her was frosty. He even refused to eat lunch with her, forcing her to either dine alone or eat with some of the clients. Fortunately,

Candace developed friends easily, and was able to get quite cozy with most of the client's accounting staff, but even that seemed to piss him off.

After two months of that crap, Candace finally went to complain to Mark McHenry, her Development Partner. Mark was assigned to her to "ensure her the best chances for success" at Y&T. Unfortunately, it was too late. Andy had already paid the partner a visit to complain about her. Apparently, Andy had told Mark that Candace was arrogant, selectively quoting from their first awful encounter, and that she was difficult to work with, couldn't handle criticism, etc. When Candace tried to explain her side of the story, including Andy's comments about Affirmative Action, his racist attitude, and Andy's obvious discomfort about working with a black female, the partner acted like she was out of her mind. "Andy's one of the most liberal guys I know," was his response. "In fact he told me that his nanny and one of his best friends are both black. Candace, I think you're just imagining things, or trying to blame Andy for your poor performance." For the Partner, that was the end of the discussion. Was Mark for real? Surely having a black nanny didn't make Andy less racist. In fact, it probably made him more so. Sure, any white boy could tolerate a black woman waiting on him hand and foot for most of his life. We all saw "Gone with the Wind." Did that mean Andy could accept a strong, smart black woman as his equal? Not a chance. And as for Andy's one black friend, did anyone ask the guy how he feels about Andy? And if he's truly Andy's best friend, he can't be a true brother, he must be a double-stuffed Oreo. While Candace didn't get the support she was looking for from Mark, what she did get was ultimately more valuable. She got clear that for her to succeed

Soul Sister's Diary

at Y&T, it would definitely be an uphill battle. She knew it was time to start playing this game full out, or leave.

Candace was seriously thinking about quitting, after all, she'd received offers from all of the big five accounting firms and she'd kept in touch with some of the Partners at Arthur Andersen and Price Waterhouse Coopers. Perhaps they'd still be interested in hiring her. She called her mom to get advice. "Candace, you know if you leave that company, its going to be just as bad at the next one. Have you forgotten we've been fighting these battles our entire lives? You can't just run away. Your father and I did not raise no quitters. Besides, remember while you were at Wharton, and that racist professor gave you Cs on all of your papers until you went to the head of the department? The department head read the papers and agreed they were 'A' work. That professor had to eat crow, and give you the grades you deserved! Well just make that Andy fella eat crow! You know you have to work twice as hard to get half as far as white people, Candace," her mother reminded her, "that's why God made you twice as smart and twice as strong."

"Yeah, mom, I hear everything you're saying. But I'm tired of fighting just to get the respect I deserve. I'm just tired period. Who needs it?"

"Just pray on it, honey. You know the lord don't give you no load to carry that's too heavy for you to bear."

"Okay mom. I love you." After Candace made the decision to stay, she began to slowly dig herself out of the hole Andy had put her in. She dug in and worked hard, clocking some serious hours. She joined the firm's flag football and bowling teams to show her loyalty and team spirit. All this career stuff sure was taking a toll on her personal life.

Michael, Candace's boyfriend of two years whom she'd met at a cookout in Michigan, began complaining that she never had enough time for him anymore. Candace knew she was lucky to have Michael; he put the 'F' in fine. He was six foot two, with smooth, chocolate skin, and a basketball player's build. Every time she looked at his ass, Candace wanted to reach out and grab it. Michael had played college basketball while at Northwestern and many people expected him to go on to the NBA. Unfortunately, he sustained a knee injury in his senior year. Fortunately, he wasn't just a dumb jock. Michael had graduated from Northwestern's engineering program with a 3.5 GPA, all while playing sports. He earned a spot at General Electric in their management-training program and was quite committed to his career. He worked some fairly long hours, which worked well at first, as he was very understanding when Candace had to work overtime.

While he was supportive at first, the more she dug into her job, the more he began to accuse her of becoming a sell-out. He wondered if she preferred the company of her white colleagues to him. While she tried to reassure him that, no, in fact, she did not prefer the company of her colleagues to him, and that all the extra-curricular activity was actually a part of her job—although not in the written job description. Michael was not convinced. Candace tried including him in the firm events so they'd be together more, but he would have none of it. "Those white boys have sticks up their asses and those white women are androgynous. Besides, Candace, it's not just your work activities. When you're not at work, you're at a NABA meeting or working at some after school tutoring program or putting on some weekend seminar for youth. I admire your commitment to the community and to black kids,

Candace, but you gotta admit it doesn't leave much room for a relationship."

"I know you don't think I have time for you Michael, but I'm doing the best that I can. The volunteering I do with the youth really brings me joy, it's the work extra-curricular activities I wish I didn't have to do. I've asked you to join the firm's football and bowling teams so we can do these activities together. Many of the significant others are on the firm's sports teams. And you know we can always use more tutors."

"Candace why would I want to join your company's sports teams? I'm not even on my company's teams. I'm already in the Big Brother program, so I don't want to add tutoring to my 'to do' list. Candace, you just need to slow down and give up some of these activities. Otherwise, we just can't make this work."

"Michael, you know I love you, but please don't ask me to do that. All of these activities are a part of who I am. I've been taught to lift as you climb, and to whom much is given much is expected. I will try to make more time for us. I just need you to be a little more patient and supportive."

"I've tried to be supportive, Candace, but for the last six months of our relationship, I've been feeling neglected. This just isn't going to work out."

So after two years, the relationship was over. Candace often wondered if she had made a mistake. She knew she had to make some sacrifices now to solidify her career, but did she also have to spend so much time working with at-risk youth? She got her answer every time she went to the Chicago Public schools and saw the despair, or helped a kid with his homework, or saw a light of inspiration in a kid's eye as she shared with them the possibilities available to them if they finished college. Although she missed Michael dearly, she knew her sacrifices were worth it, but winter in Chicago sure was cold without him!

Luckily, Candace had some close girlfriends who were making similar sacrifices for their careers. She would often get together with Lauren or Sandra Wright for moral support or just clean (and not so clean) fun. And its not like she didn't meet men, after all, at 5 ft 9in and 145 lbs., the Commodores were surely singing about her in their hit song "Brick House." She had a booty that put Brandy to shame! Still, none of the guys she met gave her the warm fuzzy feeling she had with Michael. Candace prayed every night that he missed her the way she missed him, that he would set his ego aside and be there to support her, or that he'd still be available when she got some control over her career. Candace was no fool, however. As much as she loved him, she knew there was a good chance Michael wouldn't be the one she'd end up with happily ever after.

During her second year at Y&T Candace had been assigned to work with Rob, a white guy who was actually pretty cool, on the Wilkes-Rogers account. What made Rob so easy to work with was that he basically let Candace run the audit. Rob didn't really like to work, so he'd stop by occasionally to make sure things were on track, then basically disappear for a couple of weeks. Another great thing about the Wilkes-Rogers account was that Sandra Wright had taken a job there as the Controller after she left Y&T. Sandra had become a mentor to Candace and had advised her out of some very tight spots. From then on, Candace's career had been on an upswing. The long hours and personal sacrifices had finally paid off. She was now so close to promotion to Manager that she could almost taste it. She had even called Michael the night before, and he admitted that in the two years that they'd been apart, he'd really missed her. He even asked her for a second chance. They planned to get together this weekend to talk. Candace couldn't believe it! It seemed that her dreams were all coming true!

"I'd better listen to my voice mail before I leave," thought Candace, "in case I need to stop by the office on my way home." As Candace listened to her voice mail she became increasingly stunned. She must have been a sight standing there with her mouth hanging open staring incredulously at the phone. "To erase this message, press 1; to replay it, press 2; to save it in the archives, press 3" Clearly she did not hear this message right, Candace pressed "2" to listen to the message again.

"Candace, this is John Bond." John was the partner on the Wilkes-Rogers audit. "I've just finished reviewing the audit work papers and we've got some serious issues that need to be addressed. I'm sure you well know the report is due next Friday. I'm really concerned about the work your team has done, Candace. We need to meet right away to discuss it. I'm sending a copy of this message to Rob, as well. I'll expect to see you both in my office tomorrow at 7:30 a.m., so we can begin cleaning up this mess!" "To erase this message press 1." "No", thought Candace, "I better save this one." Candace looked up to find Sandra Wright peering down at her intensely. After four grueling years at W-R, she'd finally secured the much-coveted position as the Chief Financial Officer, Candace's key client contact on the audit. From the sound of John's voice mail, Candace was once again going to need the help of her mentor.

"Didn't you hear me Candace, I said 'What's up girl?' You look seriously pressed." Sandra asked, with a sincere note of concern in her voice.

"Well, to be honest, I am. I just got a very disturbing message from the audit Partner, and I swear to you, I have no idea what he could be talking about." Candace responded.

"Well, what did he say?"

"Apparently, he just finished reviewing the audit work papers and was not impressed, to put it mildly. What I don't get is that I think we've done a great job on this audit. I tried a new approach this year, as we've discussed, which has reduced the budget substantially. As CFO you know how much pressure you guys have put on Y&T to bring the fees down. My new approach will save Wilkes-Rogers almost $20,000 in audit fees this year while increasing Y&T's realization on this audit substantially. What could have gone wrong? I gave Rob the work papers to review almost two weeks ago, and every time I asked for feedback, he said everything looked fine. Now, one week before the report is due, the partner is freaking out on me. What's that all about?"

"Smells like Houdini to me!" Candace and Sandra secretly called Rob 'Houdini' because of his tendency to disappear throughout most of the audit and mysteriously re-appear just in time to wreak havoc on his audit teams right near the deadline. "Did you do like I taught you and leave your own personal 'audit trail' to cover your ass?"

"I think so"

"Girl, you better know so!"

"I'm pretty sure I dotted all my I's and crossed all my T's. In an age of technology, with a Senior Manager like Houdini, it's almost impossible not to leave an audit trail. Let me think. At the beginning of the audit, when I had the idea to radically change the audit program, I wrote a memo summarizing my discussion with Rob and sent a copy to the partner, keeping a copy for myself, of course. In fact, since we send all correspondence by e-mail, I also have a record of when I sent all the correspondence, and when John and Rob read it. I e-mailed the audit work papers about two weeks ago, but I probably should go back and double check my log to see when Rob and John actually opened their e-mail. With respect to Rob's comments on the work papers, he left his comments, which were minimal, on my voicemail. I'm pretty sure I saved the voicemail. The only thing that could trip me up is that maybe John doesn't actually read his e-mail. Many Partners have their secretaries screen their e-mail. I could check with Gina, John's secretary, we're pretty tight. She might also be able to give me copies of any correspondence between John and Rob that I wasn't aware of."

"Well, good luck Candace, and you know I've got your back. If you need me to do anything, including talking to John and tell him what a great job Wilkes-Rogers thinks you've done, you don't have to ask twice. I sure hope they aren't trying to play you like they did Bernice and me four years ago. Surely they realize they can't get away with that crap forever. We need to call Jesse and Operation Push on their butts! I bet they're twice as devious as those boys at TEXACO. Black jelly beans indeed!"

"I for one do not intend to go out like that, Sandra. Thanks to all you've taught me, I should be ready for them." Candace replied, hoping she sounded more confident that she actually felt.

"But just in case Candace, take this." Sandra handed Candace a mini-cassette recorder. "It's voice activated and it is permissible in court! Now be sure to put in new batteries!"

"I will, and I'll call you right after the meeting to let you know how it goes."

"And just so you know, Candace, as soon as you get tired of fighting that battle, I'm sure we can find you a position here, where your talent will be recognized. It's possible that I may be able to create a position for you in my department. I'd love to have someone as smart and talented as you are on my team!"

"Thanks so much Sandra. You have been like a guardian angel to me. But I'm ready to play hardball with Y&T. I've been preparing for this battle for four years and it's about time the underdog wins one! However, if by chance I don't succeed, I'll surely take you up on your offer!"

That night Candace could not fall asleep. She kept re-playing in her mind the scene she might have to confront the next morning. She did not want to believe that these people could be so evil as to try to set her up. Damn, it was 2001, and while the firm's record on hiring and promoting African-Americans was abysmal, they already had several black Managers in other offices. What was the problem with Chicago? Rob had better not be in on this, after she'd covered for his lazy ass for the last three years while he was out playing golf, or doing lord knows what, but certainly not working on the Wilkes-Rogers audit.

When the alarm clock went off at 6:00 a.m., Candace dreaded getting out of bed. She'd hardly slept, and a look in the mirror revealed red eyes with serious luggage underneath. She quickly showered and got dressed, arriving at the office by 7:00 a.m. so she could review what John's secretary had discovered.

When Candace entered John's office at 7:25 a.m., she was surprised to find Rob already there; he was not a morning person.

Soul Sister's Diary

"Nice of you to show up Candace," Rob sneered as she entered the office. "We've been waiting almost a half hour for you."

"But the meeting wasn't supposed to start until 7:30 and its only 7:25," Candace responded defensively. These people must think she was a fool, she'd listed to John's voice mail at least ten times last night and it clearly said 7:30.

"Never mind Candace, what's important now is that you're here, so let's get started," John interjected, almost sweetly. Candace was not used to John being so cordial, clearly they had some kind of good cop/bad cop nonsense planned. This was getting interesting. "Candace, Rob told me he reviewed the work papers, almost two weeks ago, and gave you these five pages of review notes to clear, yet when I reviewed the papers yesterday, most of these items still haven't been dealt with."

So it was true. They really were trying to set her up. Candace responded as calmly as she could under the circumstances, but she really wanted to go off. "John, I never received any written review notes from Rob. I kept calling him to ask for his comments but he assured me that everything was fine, that he didn't see any major issues with the work papers," she took a deep breath to calm herself down. "Can I see the notes?" John handed Candace the notes. It was time for Candace to put Rob on the defensive. "Rob, when and how did you supposedly give me these notes? You haven't been out at Wilkes-Rogers in over three weeks." Candace knew W-R kept a log of all visitors, so this would be easy to prove. Candace enjoyed the look on John's face, apparently he didn't realize his golden boy never actually showed up at the client site, nor did he ever actually do any work.

"Rob, is this true? You haven't been out to see the client in over three weeks?"

"Um, well, um, I've had conflicting client engagements," Rob stammered, his face turning red. He was quickly losing composure. "Um, I've been pretty busy on a couple of other audits." Clearly this was not turning out how he expected.

"But Rob, you've billed W-R at least 20 hour per week for the last month. What exactly were you doing?" John, too, was now red and angry.

"Isn't this meeting supposed to be about Candace?" Rob recovered.

"Ah, yes." John shot Rob a look that let him know he wasn't completely off the hook. "Candace, what do you have to say for yourself?"

"Well, actually, Rob never answered my question. How and when did you supposedly give me these review notes Rob?"

"I e-mailed them to you a week ago Monday, Candace."

"And did your e-mail log show confirmation of my receipt?"

"I don't know."

"You mean you don't check to make sure that the e-mails you send have been opened, Rob? Isn't that standard practice? Don't bother answering that, I can save you the trouble. No, Rob, I never got the e-mail, because you never sent it." Candace asserted confidently.

"You can't prove that Candace"

"Oh, but I can. Here's a copy of my e-mail log, dating back from this morning to the beginning of the audit. And here's a copy of your e-mail log covering the same period.

Clearly, you never sent the e-mail." Candace smugly handed out copies of the e-mail logs while Rob began to sweat.

"Hey, how did you get a copy of my e-mail log?" Rob attempted, once again trying to put her back on the defensive.

"Candace, can you excuse Rob and me for about five minutes?" John interjected calmly.

"Certainly, I'll just go check my voice mail." When Candace left, she was sure to leave her briefcase, with the cassette recorder behind.

"Rob, what's really been going on at W-R? Has Candace been covering for you for three years? If that's the case, she really is one outstanding accountant."

"Okay, John, I give. I only went into the accounting field because my father was an accountant here at Y&T as was his father before him. When Candace showed up and really seemed excited about the work and was willing to work hard, I realized she didn't really need me. So I just checked in with her from time to time, and everything was fine. When you called me last week with this plan to discredit her, I didn't really agree with you, but you were so hell bent on getting rid of her, I figured if I didn't go along, you might get rid of me too. Why do you guys feel so threatened at the possibility of having a black Manager in the Chicago office? It is the new Millennium, after all."

"Rob, if we let a black become Manager, next thing you know, they'll want partnership, and they'll try to take over. Once Maurice Hill made Manager back in 1975, we had a heck of time getting him to leave quietly. He kept insisting that he deserved partnership. You should have seen the barrel of tricks we had to pull to get rid of him. My great-grandfather was a founding partner, God rest his soul and he'd roll over in his grave if he knew we let blacks become Partners. Besides, most of them just aren't Partner material. And by the way Rob, neither are you. I'll be expecting your resignation by the end of the day. How well you're compensated on the exit will depend very much on how well you play this thing out with Candace. Just stay quiet and take your lead from me."

"Whatever. We'll just see what my father has to say about this."

When she came back five minutes later, Candace was tired of this game. It was time to lay her cards on the table. After all, she had stacked the deck.

"Are you two finished yet?" Candace inquired sweetly, cautiously poking her head in the door.

"Uh, yes we are." John responded. "And I apologize Candace, clearly none of this is your fault. I've asked Rob to write a formal written apology to you as well as making him responsible for clearing both his and my review notes. I hope you'll accept my apology. I'd also like to add, Candace, that I'm supporting your promotion to Manager. You've done outstanding work on this audit and you deserve that promotion."

Surely these fools didn't think she'd be satisfied with that bone, or were they actually dumber than they looked? Now it was time for Candace to go off. She glanced down in her briefcase to make sure the recorder was still going. "I'm afraid, John, it isn't that simple." Candace started. "I think the two of you were trying to set me up."

"What? Whatever gave you that ridiculous idea?" John chuckled nervously.

"Someone anonymously left me an envelope this morning. I opened it and found Rob's e-mail log, your e-mail

Soul Sister's Diary

log, and copies of several e-mails you sent each other." Candace owed Gina big time on this one. "From what I gather, it was your idea to set me up, John. Rob was just the puppet whose strings you were pulling. It's obvious to me that this was racially motivated. What I don't understand is, how did you think you'd get away with it? Do you really think blacks are so stupid that we couldn't figure out some simple shit like this? You'll are not nearly as bright as you think you are." Candace said smugly.

Now John was hot. "If you blacks are so smart, how come we've successfully ensured that no black in the Chicago office has made it to Manager in the last 25 years? We just made a mistake thinking Rob could pull this off."

"So, you're basically admitting that this was a set up and that it was racially motivated."

"Yes, but Candace, you do realize it would be your word against mine and Rob's should you ever try to pursue this. And why would you? You'll get what you want, your promotion to Manager, and a very generous salary. I can accept defeat on this one. Frankly, I'm quite impressed with you, Candace. You're one exceptional black, if I do say so myself."

"I'm afraid I can't repay the compliment John, you're one typical insecure white man." Candace stood up, picked up her briefcase, pulled out the cassette recorder, and hit the stop button, in full view of John and Rob. As she walked out the door she paused looked over her shoulder and said "I thought you white boys were supposed to be good poker players. Surely you should have known I'd have an ace in the hole." The look on John's face was priceless!

When Candace left the office and got to the lobby, she was surprised and elated to see Michael waiting for her. "What are you doing here? It's so great to see you!"

Sandra called me last night. She told me all the crap you've been going through. I'm so sorry I haven't been there for you Candace. Do you think you can ever forgive me?"

"Well that all depends."

"On what?"

"How many carats is it worth to you? Tiffany's is just down the block"

As Michael got down on one knee, reached in his pocket and pulled out that blue box, the look on Candace's face was priceless!

Soul Sister's Diary

Ghetto Booty

When I was a young girl I was considered skinny
"You're shaped like a white girl," My sisters would tease
I would respond, "I'd rather be fat?"
Negroes, please

And I loved my body,
It was nimble and quick
I could do cartwheels, summersaults
Even Chinese splits

As I matured I kept my small waistline,
And developed hips as a teen
Firm, ample breasts a size 34 C
I was a brick house, knocked men to their knees

While away at college I by-passed the freshman 15,
Bike riding, dance and dorm food kept me quite lean.
From 123 pounds the day I walked in,
To 127 lbs. when I got my sheepskin.

But then time and life changes started to take their toll
At 25 my metabolism was no longer on a roll
I had to exercise consciously to maintain my physique,
Still I never gave a thought to what I would eat

But that was before I joined the Firm
At 26 a consultant the weight began to stick
At the end of my 2nd year I tipped the scale at 146

From dinners at restaurants with wine, appetizers and dessert,
To breakfast in bed a the Ritz Carlton
With calories and fat I'd flirt

While on a sabbatical the weight I attacked
After 2 months of diet and exercise, 135 pounds and size 8 was back.
But by age 29 my weight was officially a struggle
A roller coaster ride from 145 lbs. at its best to 160 lbs. it would bubble

For my 30th birthday I gave myself a treat
Three months of exercise and eating right
 I wore a size 8 to my party and I looked really sweet.

Now 6 years and 40 lbs. later
The skinny little girl with a white girl's shape
Has grown into a woman who is teased by her sisters
But praised by the brothers for her ghetto booty.

Soul Sister's Diary

Black

the beginning of life,
        at the fountain of creation.
        uplifting joy,
        mingled with righteous pride.
the brush of the air,
as the setting sun beckons night to its bed,
begging darkness to rest its head in the lap of daylight.
the fire of your tongue as you lick my soul.
technicolored imaginations,
        traveling to places unknown
        yet foreseen.
it is the essence of being
spiritual whirlwinds fueled by revolutionary uprisings.
droplets of water
        flowing down
        the small of my back
        the feel of the hot sand under my feet
the three eyes that rule my conscience
        follow the depth of my cypher
        to the ends of forever
the breath in the rise of your muscular chest
as you pump my blood through your veins
unified as one
with the blessings of a thousand gods
        at the crossroads of peace
and life everlasting

Soul Sister's Diary

The Struggle

Soul Sister's Diary

BLACK RAGE

Being
Labeled
Angry
Contrite
Kept

Racing
Against
Great
Expectations

THAT IS BLACK RAGE
Believing
Life
Among
Conscious
Kinfolk

Requires
Ascension
Greatness
Expressions

Towards
Overstanding
One another

THIS IS BLACK RAGE 2, BUT I AM NOT ANGRY.

Crystal Johnson, Cynthia D. Simmons, Kathy L. Andrews

CHAINS

ingrained in my mind
is that which society finds
both despicable and undesirable,
so at times, i act accordingly.

chaos amidst confusing haste
allows us to see the waste
of a thousand people walking with death
watching our lives go down.

yet by any means necessary
i must still have my dreams,
the two fists that break the chains
of my alleged criminal mind.

crystallized intelligence
strengthened with the patience
of ancient warriors,
a resurrection from the time
that binds me.

unchained, my thoughts,
like my hands are free,
opening my eyes to see
all that is mine in this world.

there are no walls to confine my expectations

which turn words into action.

Soul Sister's Diary

my life is but one minute
where faith and hope become infinite
against the circle of time.

my chain has finally broken.

Crystal Johnson, Cynthia D. Simmons, Kathy L. Andrews

Entitlement

-men are entitled to dominion over all things bright and beautiful, all creatures great and small, to put their needs before others, and to despise human weakness, although he is powerless against the tornado that carried his house and family away.

-women are entitled to dominate everything the men don't as long as we don't attempt to dominate our men. We are also entitled to nervous breakdowns because we put everyone else's needs before our own, accepting the shortcomings of our men, while having to remain perfect in mind, body, and spirit at all times.

-white men are entitled to the power that comes with everything, not limited to the house, two kids, two cars, and trophy wife, in addition to the red corvette (complete with mistress) he gets when mid-life hits.

-white women are entitled to keep looking younger by having the best plastic surgery their husband's money can buy, and when he leaves her for their neighbor's daughter, she also gets daily cocktails of vodka and Valium to block out the reality that happiness was not part of the package.

-black men are entitled to be athletes, musicians, and/or entertainers, or convicts, even though they are much more than those who fear their strength and power, and to blame their women because they are angry at themselves.

Soul Sister's Diary

-black women are entitled to be the social workers, teachers, hairdressers and single mothers angry at our black men because we loved them more than we loved ourselves.

-white people are entitled to everything (so they think) …except hip-hop, be-bop, jazz, blues, traffic lights, elevators, heart surgery, animal husbandry, fried chicken and collard greens,…the list is infinite.

-black people feel we are entitled to everything the white folks don't want, which allows us to oppress even our own folks. rejecting collectivism, embracing capitalism which undermines our individualism and our self-respect.

Crystal Johnson, Cynthia D. Simmons, Kathy L. Andrews

RESPECT TO BLACK THOUGHT

(hip-hop remix)
the freedom of our struggle can still be seen in
adidas with phat laces,
gold tooth smiles from black faces,
mixed with sanctified lyrics over syncopated beats.

Kid Capri's underground sound
brought heads from Brooklyn to the Boogie Down,
to hip the rest of the world
to the words of the street.

Cool J and Herc began puttin' in work
while DMC rapped in delight,
illustrious rhapsodies of urban life,
fake mc's and wannabees came and went,
and finally Eric B., well, he ran for president.

the Furious Five and Grandmaster stayed live.
BDP continued to thrive,
Kurtis Blow kept up the soul flow
before basketball became our only salvation.

don't forget the Treacherous Three, MC Trouble,
and Miss Me-la-dee,
Cold Crush Brothers and my peeps PE,
and Afrika Bambatta's Zulu nation…

all of a sudden the bells stopped rockin',
folks started clockin', everybody wuz jockin',

Soul Sister's Diary

threatenin' to lick a shot,
gunnin' brothers down,
sportin' hil-nigger and caps like crowns,
tryin' to grab what somebody else got.

with confusion all in our brain,
we thought we had it made, like Big Daddy Kane
we didn't take heed to the Queen's black reign,
u-n-i-t-y, must our future continue to die?

the face of hip-hop quickly changed,
labeled rap music and called deranged.
criminal delinquents simply buggin,
angry black folk just straight up thuggin'.

society labeled us violent, gangsta punks,
then vanilla ice started rhymin'
marky mark calvin kleining,
and their supposed to be the future of the funk…not!

cuz hip-hop is more than a crazy phat car,
and underpaid rap stars,
living in mansions that they rent, not own.
it's not that puff daddy pimp shit,
record industry one hits, or backstreet, blue-eyed soul

it's The Roots, De La Sol and MC Lyte,
Red Alert and Flex keep the beats tight.
we gots no time for radio station hip-hype.
Lauryn, Outkast and those kids on the hill,
Dead Prez, Mos Def, and Shao-lin keep it real.

Crystal Johnson, Cynthia D. Simmons, Kathy L. Andrews

music moguls felt hip-hop could be replaced,
Biggie and Esco keep hittin' dem wit da gas face,
They were oh so dumb, ditty-ditty dum-dum
couldn't they foretell Uncle L's phenomenon?

Soul Sister's Diary

Wannabes

To those wannabe thugs and stick-up kids,
off the slave ships to the projects, back to the pyramids,
where life once began,
golden temples of Egypt, built on hot desert sand.
Pointed directly towards the sun,
360 degrees completes our cypher of One,
a unified creation,
kings and queens of ancient Nubian nations
a fertile crescent, the moon and seven stars,
represents the significance of that which we are,
prosperous seeds sown in the banks of the Nile,
which brought forth a harvest of Man, Woman and Child.
I must bring light to the popular misconception
based on lies accepted as true perceptions,
the epitome of genocide and cultural perception.
a red, white and blue mythology,
which undermines the spirits of those like we,
a rite of passage in the nation's heartland,
supposedly life in the penitentiary creates the Black man.

while young sisters await the return of their brothers,
they are chosen to be the next welfare mothers…
at the age of sixteen,
destiny manifested as an american dream
to those unenlightened voices who may be remiss
in recognizing we grace the Earth with the blessings of Isis,
a celebration of the new black genesis
do not mistake these tall tales chosen to be facts,
that we be the sole perpetrators of negative acts,
or the fiery flames that burn in we,

Crystal Johnson, Cynthia D. Simmons, Kathy L. Andrews

are dues that were paid in cell block-c,
as graduates from the school of hard knocks,

selling our bodies as we sleep
chasing dreams in rock,
looking at life behind the barrel of a glock,
the ice, cold steel frozen blue in your hand,
has convinced you that you control the plan.
a cunning invention of colonial tricknology,
replacing the shackles of bonded slavery,
with condescending expectations that have no worth,
against the children of those who passed through the middle earth,
in floating caskets and shantytowns,
before we had ever heard of this place Capetown.
so, despite the violent efforts to overthrow us
in your god we will not trust,
cuz in the end there will be just us
to deliver the world from evil,
African roots extended through branches
of Black people.

Soul Sister's Diary

VOICES

there is a need for revolution,
at least that's what the voices tell me.
inside my head, words of injustice
explode into visions of darkness.
nat tells me of the angels he sees,
marcus speaks to his line of black stars.
words of truth will mark this sojourn.
the voices i hear make me crazy,
in this land of milk and honey.
i am entitled to everything my place has to offer
as long as that is where i stay.
so i continue to choke on the left over smoke of ism bombs,
filled with hate, not jah love,
the tears of my mothers, fathers, uncles, aunts and family
friends.
mixed with clouds of gas, creating a lethal fog.
i watched the revolution from my television,
electronic waves of struggle running through my mind,
like the heron of gil scott,
the blood of life spilled in the fields,
of my country 'tis of we.
i am armed with the wisdom of old warriors,
reminded of my militant ways,
through hushed whispers of blushing voices,
that do not know i, or from where i arrived.
my journey remains prophetic,
sheba, my queen, tells me to unite my kingdom
with the genius of her husband's word,
through the tongues of her *ghetto* children,
with their hardcore street slang,

Crystal Johnson, Cynthia D. Simmons, Kathy L. Andrews

and roughneck head bangs,
walkin' with a nickel bag of funk.
i must tell them that revolutionaries,
ain't pimps or playas hustlin' their souls
for profits.
superfly never stormed the pentagon,
or smelled the burn of napalm.
open your eyes and feel our vibes,
black power, dark like the shadows of my spirit world.
i listen and hear the old sages of my past,
my mental health wealthier than
the schizophrenic, xenophobic minds
that seek to control my knowledge.
the chain breaks with the intellect of my mind,
as i listen to my voices fearlessly,
heed their words and live their song.

Soul Sister's Diary

millenium blues
(spoken word with ink)

mother earth, there is something i must tell you.
i must tell you that your children
are suffering.

in the moment you had prepared for them many rooms,
space and time collided,
the earth stood still while the ocean kissed the sky,
leaving a trail of tears
that has plagued you prosperity since birth.

(louder)
in cuba they cried.
in selma they cried.
in natchez, missippi they cried.
in hanoi they cried. in cambodia they cried.
(faster)
in angola, botswana and uganda they cried.

iwroteitdown, iwroteitdown, iwroteitdown,
i roared it down, like a lioness i roared it down
rivers i have known through streams of consciousness,
so loud that even the shadow dwelling
in the valley of death
would read my mind and not forget.
bombs bursting in mid air
rocket missiles with red glare
giving proof to the night
the contempt we all share.

Crystal Johnson, Cynthia D. Simmons, Kathy L. Andrews

o say does that bullet riddled banner yet wave
in the land of the free, but the home of the….slave?
inexcusable red, white and brutalities
blood blotched ink stains on
turning pages of history.
so it is written as it was done.

and mother they still cried. (lamenting)
in south africa, for biko they cried.
in beirut they cried.
in tianamen they cried.
in belfast and dublin they cried.
in nicaragua y por los desaparecidos they cried.
in los angeles they cried….

so again,
iwroteitdown, iwroteitdown, iwroteitdown,
i roared it down streetcorner alleys,
over spray painted walls of heirograffiti,
prophetic visions of the weak and needy,
and the huddled masses are still tired and hungry.

despair now lines the pockets of
philosophical indifference and political unrest.

so if things come apart at the seams,
if things really fall apart by what seems,
seems like the apple has fallen
much to far from the tree.

when did the breath above our heads
become someone's air space?

Soul Sister's Diary

when did stories told in sea waves
become international waters?
are we feng shui or sinn fein?
just us, our selves alone?

so in the moment it takes a village to bomb a child
any child, anywhere
i wield my pen like the adversarial sword
cutting through the chaos and corruption
to right.
to rightthewrongs, iwriteitdown,
iwriteitdown torightthewrongsiwriteitdowntowritethewrongs

a cunning invention of ship splitting submarines and wounded
knees.
shattered nuclear arms, bodies hung from trees,
with literary logic that outwits new millenium mathematics.

(rapid run on)

**if.a.steamroller.bulldozing.an.african.village.travels.at.the
same.rate.of.speed.as.a.pickup.truck.with.a.caged.byrd
chained.to.its.wheels.which.is.three.times.the.number.of
seconds.it.takes.a.bomb.to.explode.in.the.catholic.provinces
of.ireland.times.the.sum.of.the.number.of.sticks.and.stones
hurled.at.israeli.soldiers.in.the.west.bank.divided.by.the
number.of.indonesian.uprisings.plus.medical.embargos.to
countries.afflicted.with.super.power.syndrome.multiplied
by.the.square.root.of.united.nations.military.coup.of
dictatorship.setup.and.sponsored.by.them,**

Crystal Johnson, Cynthia D. Simmons, Kathy L. Andrews
❦

then just how many times does forty-one go into one?

fred hampton would tell you then, what amadou would say now,
if he could.
aaah, but i digress.
mr. horowitz has raised an interesting point, yes
can reparations really repair nations
burned and looted by babylon?

so mother i must tell you,
your children still cry.

in gaza they cry.
in rwanda they cry.
in the congo they cry.
in pakistan they cry.
in cincinatti they cry.
in new york they cry.

but in remembrance i write.
iwriteitdowntorightthewrongsiwriteitdowntorightthewrongs.
(lather, rinse, repeat)

Soul Sister's Diary

Public Safety

Dedicated in Memory of Amadu Dialo and the many who fell before him, and to those who will give their lives in justice.

You have the right.
You have the right to remain silently still, as I
Emotionally, mentally, and physically abuse your soul.
Anything you say can and will be
Disregarded,
Disbelieved,
And eventually discredited.
All because
You look like somebody,
Who looks like somebody,
Who looks like somebody.
You will be allowed one phone call,
Do you know who to reach out and trust?
You have the right to a proper defense.
Since I know you can not afford a slick,
Overpaid, under-worked attorney,
One will be provided.
An overworked, underpaid defender of public opinion,
Will convince you to bargain for your life,
By pleading with the merciless court,
for your innocence.
If you are not guilty now, you will be later
So let due process begin in this moment.

Crystal Johnson, Cynthia D. Simmons, Kathy L. Andrews

You also have a right to be judged by a jury of my peers
Who know nothing of you or you beginnings,
Yet at my word,
They will despise you and everything for which you stand,
As you spend the next 6 months in captivity
Waiting for the speedy trail guaranteed by my constitution.
You have the right to remain angry
Cloaked in constant rage,
At how easy it is for me to,
Cut corners,
Harass individuals,
Cover my ass,
Renounce my spirit,
And degrade my humanity.
All with the blessing of those superiors,
Who expect me to do my job and make them look good.

Although I am sickened by what I have created,
I am here to protect the peace,
Although you have none.
This is public safety, only we are not safe.
You have the right to be joyfully disgusted, as you read of my demise,
At my own hands, hands which shackled your serenity,
crafted your ruins, and kept you down.
So as you sit and think of me from the narrow cell that resembles my mind,
you have the right to remain silent.

Soul Sister's Diary

Spirituality & Healing

Crystal Johnson, Cynthia D. Simmons, Kathy L. Andrews

THE THIRD "I"

mystically envisioning
the secret path of life
that lies behind me
in front of me
with me at all times.

as i ascend to the darkness
that brings forth life
the flow on ancient rivers
travel through the
canals of my mind.

Soul Sister's Diary

CRUCIFIXION

Her soul is trapped on the tail of a majestic desert wind
Spinning tumultuously, to the extent that each grain of sand
Denotes the passage of time
Through the hourglass of her identity.
memories of her glory
a plight upon civilizations colonized by corruptive caucasian consciousness.
Time is not on her side,
So she travels lifelessly through the ages,
Attempting to secure her space on the continuum of the living.
Catching up leads to being caught up, so caught up in the tornado that has twisted her,
inside out
upside down
every which way but loose from the stake that mounts her to the ground she swore to protect.
Cuz down here on the ground, ain't no place to be livin'.
She has trouble rising from the ashes,
Set down amongst the burnt offerings of bablylonian nightmares,
To reap the wages of the sins against humanity.
Remaining in bondage long after she is supposed to be free.

Long after Isis gave her first born to the sun
Long after her children were stolen shamelessly from her bosom
Long after Black Moses recreated the flow of the Nile, liberating her peoples in the land of false promises
Long after the rings around the necks of her menfolk
Mirrored the years of the trees that bore their fruit.

Long after the sha-clak-clak, sha clak-clak, the sha clak-clak
reminds brother Saul
where his niggaz be at.
Long after what was supposed to be her salvation.

Still she remains upon the cross,
held down by the five points of a star that will never shine
with the revelations of revolution.
on the day
god gave his only begotten son, He sacrificed his mother, and
disowned his only daughter,
choosing to reap praise upon a holy ghost
a deified apparition that is a glaring aberration upon her spirit.
Despite the nonbelievers
from the church of the poison minds
She sings the songs of the voodoo priestess,
Her high pitched yell, a conduit for the conjurer calling to the
ancestors,
Raising los santos de Santeria
Passing through the deep cobalts and indigo midnights of
Yemaya
Seven shades of seven tribes across seven seas,
Swept ashore with the healing lamentations of great-great-
great grandmothers
Talking with drums and speaking in tongues,
Conversations carried in the haze of a purple fog, resting in
the laps of Southern bayous,
Embedded in the round the way beats of the urban bush people,
Echoed over the roof top barrios of the concrete jungle,
From the four corners of the global ghetto,
Her voice still rings, and
in my mind she sings…

The Lake

The lake brings me peace of mind like no other body. I can share my deepest secrets with the lake without the fear of being judged. The lake is my friend and counselor.

By the lake I watch people walking. I see their life story in their eyes. I sense their current moods in their steps.

By the lake in the distance, I see rolling hills, cotton candy clouds and birds taking wing. The sunshine bounces off my body, slings me back to life, brings me back to the light.

I take in the fresh air, smell the grass and feel the cool breeze off the water tickle my skin. The lake's tiny waves dance and the sun glistens.

One day I'll be well known – near famous for the things that I do on this earth. Many people will appreciate my deeds. But I appreciate nothing more than the lake's calming affect on my soul.

God placed this lake here for me to admire and trust. Trusting myself is sometimes hard to do. Factors like doubt, anxiety, low self-esteem, and ignorance of my greatness stops me from moving forward, taking the risk to make a difference. The lake is my friend and counselor. It makes a difference; it knows its greatness.

Crystal Johnson, Cynthia D. Simmons, Kathy L. Andrews

In God's Hands

You spend most of your life taking the high road. Putting everyone's feelings and needs before your own. Where does it get you?

Everyday my elders teach me how to make it to heaven by being a good person. They've taught me things that have helped me to become someone who is special, thoughtful, caring, kind and destined to reach the stars. They have the wisdom and knowledge that only decades of living can give you. But I've lived a couple of decades myself. After getting used again and again, after reflecting on why and how I managed to come out the loser every time, I began to wonder if there isn't some other way.

Life is beautiful, especially when you have positive, thoughtful and kind people in your life, people you can count on to put your needs and feelings right up there with their own. These people are the backbone of your existence. They make you feel like your on top of the world, especially when you are at your lowest.

God has given me only a few of those special souls; I can count them all on one hand. I am fortunate enough to have plenty of people who care for and love me, but only a select few I can count on. Those individuals know me inside out and have done wonderful things for me, even though I didn't ask. Those few beautiful souls would never let me go hungry or without shelter. They would give me the shirt off their backs. They would give me the blood from their veins.

Soul Sister's Diary

Love is wonderful, but love and intimacy is heavenly. I would love to have earthly heaven. The heaven you possess when you look into your man's eyes and feel what he feels. My elders haven't taught me how to get that piece of heaven.

So many chances at intimacy and love have passed by my door, but none have made a home in my heart. Sometimes, I feel doomed to find my greatness and to have no one to share it with. There is a reason for this loneliness I can't see or understand right now. After three decades of living, is it too much to ask for a special partner to adore and who adores me? I'm trying my best to be patient.

"Put it in God's hands", the elders say. I keep repeating that mantra, convincing other lonely souls that there is truth in that chant. There is truth in that chant. I believe I will put it in God's hands.